DARK

PSYCHOLOGY

AND

MANIPULATION

How to Analyze and Influence Anyone with
Body Language, **NLP**, and **Gaslighting**

LUCAS BAILEY

Your FREE Bonuses

Download the following eBooks for free to
supplement your learning.

Bonus 1: Understanding Mind Control

Discover

- Why mind control and brain washing works
- Who is susceptible
- How to deal with manipulators
- ...and more

Bonus 2: 7 Proven Keys to Persuade

Discover

- How to offer an irresistible deal
- How to create a sense of urgency
- Create a strong call to action
- ...and more

Scan the QR Code below to gain access:

Dedicated to my life's mentor and the greatest man I know. This one's for you Dad.

Contents

DARK

PSYCHOLOGY

AND

MANIPULATION

INTRODUCTION

Why did this book catch your eye? Do you want to get a leg up on everyone else in this world, do you want to make more friends, or have you been manipulated in the past?

Whatever the reason, knowing how to read people and what makes them tick is bound to help. Trying to change an opinion or behavior is a difficult process. Humans are stubborn and, now more than ever, are extremely attached to their beliefs and can't fathom that they have bias.

Knowing how to approach people, what behaviors to look out for, and how to work your way to the right solution will keep you safe and help you get what you want. It's not all sunshine and rainbows. You will also be confronted by how these methods have caused irreparable damage. Will this book teach you how to start a cult or swindle millions out of people, maybe if you are the right (or wrong) person? Hopefully, you will come out of it with a better grasp on people, society, and even yourself.

Dark Psychology Sounds So Cynical Though, Can't We Just Be Nice?

The idea of not taking people at their spoken word and relying on psychological tricks and body language sounds gross. It flies in the face of everything we are taught as children, to be open, honest, and trusting. It is predicated on the world being as decent and fair as we think, but that is a fantasy. Everyone has to be out for themselves to some extent, or else we would put all our retirement savings into the first charity we see. We would never pursue anyone romantically, compete or succeed.

It's a bitter pill, but trusting people outright will only blind you. Most people are good, but people can make mistakes that can harm you or fall in with the wrong crowd. Our society is almost entitled to trust. Potentially going out of your way to vet someone can lead to defensiveness, not just because they might be hiding something, but the implication of distrust is seen as a judgment of character. There are certain behaviors and times where you should take a person at their word, but you always need to be asking questions.

2

We give away trust too freely in the effort to be approachable or friendly in this world. While a person that does this can forge more friendships, people can take advantage and see it as a weakness. Once you invite the wrong person into your life, they will stick to you like gum at the bottom of a shoe.

Before we start, just know you shouldn't advertise these skills.

You might want to say:

- *You scratched your nose. You are lying!*

- *I can read your mind!*

- *I am great at reading people!*

- *I can spot liars a mile away!*

- *I am a great liar!*

At best, people might think you are full of it, but at worst, people might start being careful around you. They will be more guarded, rehearse their lies, and watch their body language more.

A lot of methods can be fooled with practice and decent counters, and you have set yourself up for receiving lousy information. By all means, tell people that this was a good read, but don't brag about your skills. Above all else, you should leave here realizing that discretion can be a gift.

Why Are You Here?

Really think about what you want to get out of this book. While many tips are framed in certain situations, you can use them in many ways. From getting hired, to convincing a spouse to agree with you, even to hurt others. How you interpret the information, the stories, and the lessons will reflect you. Think of it as a knife; you can hurt people or bring them joy by using it to cook.

HOW TO ANALYZE ANYONE

"You cannot not communicate: Every behavior is a form of communication. Because behavior does not have a counterpart (there is no anti-behavior), it is not possible not to communicate."

– PAUL WATZLAWICK

Nonverbal communication is the first and most important form of information that a person transmits usually without even being aware of it. As the old adage goes "you cannot not communicate". The truth is humans are terrible at hiding their intentions, and if someone can read the signs it puts them at a tremendous advantage.

Nonverbal communication is essentially everything we say without words—our body language, how we dress, our tone, our cadence, and our facial expressions. You can tell so many things about a person before the utterance of "Hi, my name is-."

Let's start simple. You are about to enter a store, and you see the person at the front desk slouching, looking pouty, and texting. That representative can be the best in the business, but because of the initial impression you got from them outside the store, they will never have the chance to prove it.

We learn this as infants. When our mom smiled and spoke in a higher pitch, we knew things were great. We learned to fear when mom yelled, looked angry, or away. Infants need that sort of communication to thrive. A mother can keep them fed and cleaned, but the infant will quickly become distressed if they do not engage with physical signs of love and affection. They will try to engage the mother with gestures and laughter, then cry, then, in time, they give up and self-soothe. Nonverbal communication is so crucial to our development that infants will not thrive and can develop lifelong problems even if all their physical needs are met. This can be seen in large orphanages. Babies have their physical needs met but not the emotional ones because there is insufficient staff. Adoptive parents report that these babies sometimes don't cry when first adopted. Instead, they rock back and forth, chewing on their clothes–anything to self-soothe. This needs professional intervention, but kids sometimes develop attachment disorders and anxiety and learn to cope with drugs. Rarely do those years of reinforcing that they cannot rely on anyone to help them can lead to antisocial behavior.

We grow, and through socialization, we learn how to read our surroundings without anyone having to say a word. Our parents and teacher correct us on our posture, told us we are wearing a sour face, and told us to uncross our arms because we look "angry."

Humans for the most part rarely control or filter their body language and nonverbal cues. For those who know what to look for, salespeople, lawyers, police, and therapists can use body language to tailor their strategies and help a person feel at ease. With some awareness, you can read between the words and analyze anyone and their plans for you.

Debunking Body Language Myths

Many bloggers and "experts" watch too many crime dramas and have a flawed notion of what nonverbal communication is and isn't. For one, it is not an exact science. Many mitigating factors can affect a person's nonverbal communication. Culture is a huge one. In western cultures, prolonged eye contact is endearing. Many Asian cultures find it rude. Kissing acquaintances and remaining in close proximity are common in Latino and a few European cultures. In some Northern European cultures, being that close or casual with a stranger is inconceivable. Anxiety and sensory overstimulation can also affect the gaze. For someone like this, prolonged eye contact can be exhausting, and in trying to think, it is easier to look away or close your eyes. Autistic individuals may not have the same nonverbal communication style since this comes with socialization.

One of the most significant body language myths is that averting the gaze means that a person is lying. This is simply not true, and there are many reasons why a person could look away. There is also the misconception that certain self-soothing gestures are indicative of dishonesty. Self-soothing gestures are just that; they are ways we comfort ourselves when we are particularly overstimulated or stressed. Touching the hair, rocking, and even crossing the arms are considered self-soothing.

The biggest trap many "body language experts" fall into is connecting anything other than openness as a signal of dishonesty. Frowning, covering the mouth, folding arms, or touching the nose, are often labeled smoking guns. These should be thought of as signs of stress, but that does not equate to lying. The person might not be comfortable talking to a stranger; they may be stressed about something else or are stressed out at the notion of being questioned.

When people are on defense, they subconsciously close themselves off or self-soothe. People don't trust they will be believed, and our body language can create a self-fulfilling prophecy.

If you're interested in truly reading somebody you have to look at the big picture. Body language analysis can be misinterpreted even by the best. That is why you have to look at a person's baseline, verbal communication, and the facts presented in front of you.

Becoming a Mind Reader Using Nonverbal Communication

The most successful people look at the person they are interacting with and infer a million things without exchanging words. Our nonverbal communication and communication style can betray many intentions our words attempt to hide. Looking at the big picture can help you navigate people you may need something from, who you work with, and who may try to hurt you.

The Importance of Posture and Body Language

Let's take our interactions with people and examine them in layers. A person's overall shape is a reflection of their posture. Posture can subconsciously tell a person so much. Posture communicates hierarchy, confidence, and health. Surprisingly when it comes to conveying bigger emotions, the body can reveal much more than the face.

In pop culture, no one embodies the importance of posture more than Superman. Despite being the same person, Superman makes Clark Kent look meek and soft. In the 1973 *Superman* movie, Christopher Reeves demonstrates this brilliantly. As Clark Kent, slouches, hides behind glasses, can be clumsy and looks slightly disheveled, and speaks in a nasally voice. As Lex Luthor put it, "he is a parody of a man in comparison." In the same scene, without changing into his costume, he becomes Superman. He stands tall, speaks clearly and deeply, and is not afraid to take up space. The audience can not believe why such a weak attempt at hiding his identity works; no one would think that someone who looks that unsure of himself could be the pinnacle of strength.

In a new environment, you can quickly determine the hierarchy with posture. Confident leaders don't need to default to displaying strength. The mistake people make is they interpret rugged masculinity and intimidation as leadership. They will stand with their chest puffed out, standing so straight they look like they have a back brace on, and do everything in their power to make the other person feel small. When you communicate aggression right off the bat, people tend not to trust you.

Look at proven leaders. They are often relaxed and are not afraid to take up space because they know their status in the room. At a podium, they stand up straight with their shoulders rolled back. They look confident but not stiff like they are standing at attention. If a person is nervous but trying to stand up straight, they may forget that they can move their arms or have a white knuckle grip on the podium.

Women are much more in tune with body language than men. Some men are baffled as to why women don't respond well even if they said everything right. A lack of confidence is the kiss of death for a man flirting; women can sense it with body language a mile away. Slouching, head down, hands in pockets, blocking with a drink, or not being squared with another person are all signs of a lack of confidence. This is a submissive pose because an animal does its best to look smaller. Think about being in a bar and choosing who you will spend your precious time with. Plus, think about it, which of these guys looks more fun?

The cultural perception that men cannot read signals from women is based on scientific fact. In FMRI studies analyzing nonverbal communication, women's brains lit up brighter and more than men's when analyzing body language. Simply, women dedicate more brain power to nonverbal cues than men. There are so many stories of men missing obvious hints that a woman is attracted. Women have plenty of behaviors that can signal attraction. Preening, or adjusting clothes that are otherwise fine, flipping her hair, exposing the neck, standing square with a man, the absence of blocking with a purse or drink, and leaning in to talk can be signs that a woman is attracted. Some women may engage in *parading.* This is when she walks in a way where she swings her hips, back arched, chest out, and stomach in. As the bond grows, she may be comfortable; women might feel more comfortable and initiate contact by touching her thigh to a man's or touching foot to foot.

Men can be oblivious to the fact that women are uncomfortable in a situation just by their body language. Women will have all the classic signs. They will close themselves off by keeping distance, crossing their arms and sometimes their legs, averting their gaze, and blocking themselves off with any available object. If you are at a bar and a woman is doing any of these, stop engaging and move on. Women may feel too uncomfortable with direct confrontation and use humor or gently let you down. But, their body language can tell you everything that their subconscious is screaming out.

Body language can convey power, emotions, and intentions, but it is only the first part of effective reading.

Use Sleight of Hand to Get People's Attention

Hand movements when you talk are integral to making a compelling argument. Humans are visual creatures, and hand movements are very pleasing to us. If you look at TED talks or politicians, they all have hand movements mastered. It is like a dance, graceful but not over the top.

Notice that when we stick our hands up with our palms out to concede a point or try to calm someone down, that's no accident. Open palms convey trust by letting a person know you are not hiding anything.

To convey a message effectively, hand movements must maintain a delicate balance. Some gestures like pointing should be avoided, one because it can be offensive in cultures but also because it looks accusatory and is considered rude even in the west. Politicians tend to keep the thumb pressing on their index finger or open palm/slightly curled fingers for emphasis. Remember not to overdo this. Keep the hands folded close to the body in calmer moments. Then when you really want to emphasize a point, you can chop the palm. Remember, if everything is important, then nothing is. This can be a difficult skill to master, but with practice and a little modeling, you can pull it off next time you give a big talk.

Dress for the Job You Want

Our clothes tell people a lot about our state of mind, attitudes, and values and have a ton of power. A lab coat automatically instills a sense that the person in question has a place in authority and is intelligent and trustworthy. Clothes can reveal the power, a desire for respect or vulnerability, which can be advantageous in different circumstances. Men's formal attire imparts masculinity, power, and respect. Business attire in women can read a bit more masculine for the same effect. However, a delicate balance must be struck. If a woman is perceived as too masculine based on what she wears, her peers can see her as problematic or combative.

Universally people look favorably at clothes that:

- Are clean
- Fit well
- Are pressed
- Are appropriate for the setting

- Are either currently in fashion or timeless
- Look well-made
- Are flattering to the body

If any of these are missing, it doesn't matter what brand or how expensive your clothes are. People will perceive you negatively.

The first thing to look at is cleanliness. Clothes that are dirty, wrinkled, don't fit, or torn can leave someone thinking you are a slob, careless, or poor. Unfortunately, as much as we want to pretend our society is not shallow, it is simply not the case. A person who shows up to a job interview with a wrinkled shirt or pants with a coffee stain on them would most likely not get the job because it signals to the employer that they do not care enough about the position to put their best foot forward. They can answer every interview question correctly, but a judgment has already been made based on the clothes. Corporate clothing tends to lean more conservatively, with most of our skin covered and shirts buttoned high. The goal is to be universally appealing to any client that walks through the door. Any deviance from that can imply a level of casualness that may not be a part of company culture.

Clothes play a massive role in courtship. Society conditions women to look their best at events and for potential partners. They are allowed more creativity and options in clothes, one of their most important means of self-expression. In their dating app pictures, their first picture will be of them in a nice outfit, with hair and makeup done. Women, more often than not, dress up for first dates to give the best first impression. Men tend to choose mates based on their perceived availability and appearance. Therefore women work hard to look nice and primed for social events.

Men can be blind to this and can suffer in the dating world. Putting effort into one's appearance can be seen as feminine and shallow. Men try to look effortlessly handsome or forgo the concept altogether, thinking it should not matter. They often put little to no effort into their pictures and wonder why their blurry nightclub photos or car selfies do not yield results. Unfortunately, this is where the respective socialization of the sexes can lead to conflict. Men often say they "hate makeup," although the woman in question is wearing multiple products to pull off no makeup. They also tend to be the ones who show up to dates looking unprepared, wearing athletic shorts, t-shirts, and inappropriate shoes. Meanwhile, women take the time to look perfect and can become self-conscious if they miss an element such as nails or hair. A perceived lack of effort on a man's part can signal to a woman that he is not putting in action and is not worth pursuing.

While clothes can communicate professionalism, authority, and attraction, they can also be used strategically to show vulnerability. Nowhere is this more evident than in trials. The need to dress up for court is not just because courtrooms notoriously blast the AC; it can be a great way to impart a perception to the jury. You may notice that defendants in the courtroom dress far differently than their pictures portray. Defendants rarely take the stand when a murder trial is involved, mainly because there is little upside. They have the right not to incriminate themselves, and if they appear nervous or defensive while answering questions, the jury may interpret that as lying. They often have to communicate nonverbally, starting with the clothes.

The Menendez brothers' trial had a genius method of shaping the jury's perception (at least in the first trial). The defense was that the boys acted in self-defense because their father had been abusing them. There was just one problem. These were full-grown men in their twenties by the time they went to trial. A jury would have difficulty believing that a much older man could abuse these men. Instead of suits, the defense had the brothers dress in sweaters to portray vulnerability and immaturity. The strategy resulted in a hung jury.

This vulnerability can backfire in most circumstances. This is common with tourists. When going anywhere unfamiliar, it's best not to stand out. Telegraphing you are an outsider also means you are naive and probably carrying a lot of cash. It can make you a target for scams, pickpockets, and groups with much more nefarious purposes. Also, locals may negatively perceive tourists; they may be less willing to help or be wary of you. This is not limited to Americans. Any culture can fall into similar versions of these tropes. Some items that scream tourist include:

- Baseball hats (a team is a dead giveaway you might not be local)

- Sports jerseys

- Obviously, branded clothing or shoes (just because a brand is ubiquitous in your country does not make it common in other countries)

- Conspicuous sunglasses

- Athleisure

- Depending on the country; bright colors and patterns

- Bulky and often new sneakers

- Fanny packs or overpacked wallets

- Lots of luggage or a colossal backpack

- University attire

- Not being prepared for the weather

It would behoove you to do a bit of research to see what clothes are customary where you are visiting. For example, in Germany, dark and neutral colors are standard as opposed to loud clothing. In Paris, athleisure would mark you as a hedonist. In New York, an *I Love New York* shirt will get you harassed by the man in the Elmo costume and people giving out mixtapes. You also want to keep the bulk down as much as you can. Use a money belt to hide cash and your ID. Leave the giant camera at home unless necessary. Take up as little room as possible and try and ask yourself what your outfit can tell people. You want to give as little information as possible.

Lack of a Poker Face

When people think of nonverbal communication, the first thing they default to is the face, and with good reason. Facial expressions can tell us a lot from a reasonable distance, emotions, health, stress, alertness, and intoxication, to name a few. It is also where more reliable cues are obvious since humans evolved to read and express very minute facial changes. Scientists posit that facial expressions are not cultural, passed down from early humans and developed through selective pressure. There is a lot to back this up; for example, smiling is ubiquitous in humans when they are happy. Blind individuals will emote the same as seeing individuals despite having no frame of reference. It was so advantageous that domesticated dogs developed muscles in their eyes to better connect to humans.

Since we cannot see our own faces, we end up giving away a lot more than we mean. The face is where a lot of *desynchronization* happens. This is the disconnect between what someone is telling you and what they look like. Consider this, you screw up, and you have to tell someone; you ask them if they are mad, but to not hurt your feelings, they say no. You can automatically tell they are lying because they look tense and frowning. Humans not only find this off-putting but, in some cases, creepy since it deviates from how we expect those in our species to communicate.

If we break down the face, we can start to notice patterns that can point to stress (once again, these are points of interest, not necessarily a smoking gun). Sometimes the story in the face deviates from the story coming out of the mouth.

Body Language Can Be Skin Deep

The skin is the largest organ in the body, and since most of its functions are entirely out of a person's control, it can make for a reliable read. Things to look out for are:

- Paleness

- Sweat

- Rosiness

- Lack of hygiene

Lack of hygiene can tell you something. Some of these can be health related. A pale and sweaty person is not doing well health-wise, even if they insist they are okay. Other signs can scream discomfort or stress from a mile away. Some people become very rosy when stressed or embarrassed, and this is not limited to the cheeks. Discoloration can spread to the ears and neck. It's an excellent place to look if a girl is wearing makeup. Also, look for slips in hygiene. If someone who is normally put together comes in with gunk in their eyes or crumbs around their mouth, their mind could be somewhere else, and they don't realize that they look off.

Look Into My Eyes

Eye contact is a powerful thing. They are the window to the soul for a good reason. When you notice someone is making direct eye contact with you, your autonomic nervous system is aroused, you perk up, become self-conscious, and are way more judicious in your actions. We get annoyed when we are explaining something to someone, and they start staring off into space because it indicates they are not paying attention. Eye contact is so ingrained in us that even if a person is looking right at us, if they don't have what can only be described as a "sparkle" in their eyes when listening, we can tell that the information did not quite reach their brain. You see this often if a person is tired, drunk, or bored. If you look closely, the pupils can provide some decent hints. Pupils dilate when you are stressed or aroused.

Your eyes give away where your attention is and your emotions. It's why poker players wear sunglasses during indoor games. Any little tell can give rivals a mountain of information in a game as strategic as poker. They might see you staring at the deck, looking at others' cards, eyeing your cards for too long, or see your eyes widen at a certain point in the game.

The brows are also a treasure trove of information. When a person is stressed, the first place it shows up is in the brows when they furrow. It is so prevalent that a sign of aging and stress is the development of permanent frown lines that can only be treated with Botox.

Eyes are also a dead giveaway if a person is happy or not. It is easy to put on a smile to try and fit in or not give away your state of mind. That smile rarely travels to the eyes if it is not genuine. It can lead to an uncanny valley effect that is unappealing to look at. Once again, this is a massive issue in dating that men are unaware of.

So, let's say you are putting together your new profile, but you realize you don't have many photos. Men are not as socialized to take photos as women. They may not get the chance or find the whole exercise frivolous in their need to be masculine. Since they are not used to photos, they may get nervous looking at the camera and feel self-conscious about this moment getting immortalized in someone's cloud drive, but they try to hide it with a smile. The result is a stack of off-putting photos screaming, "this is not my real personality."

You now have a profile of you pretending to be happy instead of engaging in activities that make you happy. You may say, "well, I do have hobbies that make me happy, but I don't need to photograph that; I like to live in the moment." Fine, that may be true, but these are picture-based apps, and you must think of the message you are sending. An excellent way to get your smile to be genuine if you need one good selfie is to listen to something you find genuinely funny. It can be a standup routine or a podcast, just something where you know you will laugh.

Wait for the joke, laugh, then smile and take the shot. The smile will travel to your eyes and beats a selfie in a dirty bathroom mirror every time.

Watch Your Mouth

Besides the eyes, the mouth is the most animated part of the human face. We all know that smiling and frowning are universally code for happiness and sadness—the act of smiling only tells part of the story. If a smile is forced, it can look extremely unnatural, and there are a few easy tells. A closed-lip smile, crooked smile (unless the person is having a stroke), a smile without an arch, or a smile that is only limited to the mouth always look dishonest or, at the very least uncomfortable. Just keep in mind that some people might just have a weird smile, tooth trouble, or dentures that can affect their smile.

The mouth is a treasure trove of micromovements that people are unaware of. Biting or licking the lips can indicate stress. Pursing the lips can mean disapproval. Pouting can mean defiance or can even be flirty under certain circumstances.

When you drop a revelation or catch someone in a lie, see if their jaw drops even just a little. Most people can't help but relax their jaw a little when they are taken aback by something. If they are skeptical or confused, they might tick their jaw muscle or twitch their lip to the side. This might be the only micro expression they leak before lying to your face to appease you.

Don't Just Hear, Listen

Listening to someone speak is not just about the words; it's the tone, inflection, and volume of words. First, listen to the volume, especially changes in volume. When people get defensive or stressed, they naturally raise their voices. Pitch is also a big one. People may resist raising their voices but often forget to relax their vocal cords. The result is a higher pitch that is not very convincing to the average person.

A slightly uncomfortable but telling sign of stress is a lot of clicking saliva sounds in the mouth. Stress and anxiety can cause a person's mouth to dry up. You see plenty of water in televised hearings and courtrooms. If a person has not been talking long and goes to take several sips of water, that can be a sign that they are massively stressed out.

Tone also needs to be analyzed. Granted, this can vary by age group and culture. Still, in the west, some consistencies align with confidence. Make sure not to up-talk. This is when a person ends a statement with an upper inflection like they are asking a question. It might work for entertainers on social media, but in a formal setting, it just makes you sound unsure.

You might already be stressed, and your body is freaking out. The last thing you want to do is keep your lungs from working efficiently. Breathe, and stand up

25

straight. Good posture does not only make you look confident but sound confident. Ensure that the effort to speak comes from your lungs, not your throat.

Finally, there is the cadence or the rhythm of your speech. When panicked, stressed, or lying, some people will talk very fast, leaving no room to breathe. This makes for lousy communication since the other person cannot digest what is being spoken to them. There is also too much hesitation in inappropriate places, leading to awkward pauses and a confused audience. The best orators have a consistent cadence, with breaks in select parts. This can let the audience digest the main idea or give them room for an emotional reaction.

Creating a Good First Impression: Job Interviews

Body language is a great way to give yourself an edge while job hunting. Unfortunately, your resume and technical ability will only get you so far. Think of the HR manager as a mid-level boss you have to fight to get to the princess, aka a lucrative job. HR managers may not have the know-how to understand the nuances of the job you are applying for. What they are looking for is if you will fit into the culture. Unless you are deliberately scouted, the onerous is on you to convince them you are suitable for the company. This means you must put on your best *ideal sociable employee* mask for the interview. If you are shy or just hate people, you need to pretend that you are confident and extroverted for that 30-minute interview.

It all starts with a presentation.

- Never take risks with clothes; dress professionally and conservatively (obviously, this depends on if the environment is corporate or casual). Stay away from loud patterns and colors. You want the interviewer to remember what you said and not be known as "that orange guy." An older HR manager may frown on any deviation from the norm.

- Maintain an open and positive disposition even if you are nervous. Maintain eye contact, and be conscious of self-soothing behaviors such as tapping or leg bobbing. Keep your arms uncrossed and your hands visible. This may take some practice, but it is vital. You never want to give someone a reason to reject you, even if they do so unconsciously.

- Keep the interviewer's body language in mind. If they are relaxed, you can relax a bit. Be wary if they are in a bad mood. They may unintentionally reflect that in their body language, and you might end up mirroring them. Since mirroring is unconscious, they will blame you for the uncomfortable disposition in the room.

- Be an active listener and mirror what they say about the job and the company. Body language can help convey this. Lean forward slightly and nod when you sense something important is being said.

- This one might hurt but laugh at their jokes. It's an easy way to get them on your side. You can boost their ego without having to suck up to them directly. If they talk about their personal life, pretend to be interested and ask a follow-up question.

- Successful interviews are a two-way street so ask questions. Most importantly, ask the interviewer their opinion about the company and what they think it takes to be successful. The earlier you do this, the better because you can parrot those traits back to them when you...

- Emphasize how you will benefit them, i.e., the company. What specifically do you bring to the table? Remember, you are a team player, technically qualified (your resume already dictates that), who is also capable of working on your own. Bring out tangible results from previous jobs to emphasize your point. Do not humble brag. Your accomplishments must be framed around the interview, not so much you. Humble bragging is easy to spot, and interviewers hate it.

- Emphasize that you are there for the long haul if they ask how long you plan to stick around. Don't even joke about quitting early. Your answer is not a binding contract, so even if you only plan on staying a year, never mention that unless it's a temporary gig. No one wants to waste resources training someone who will leave before another candidate.

Is some of this deceptive? Yes, but it is easier to land the job and then slip off the mask a bit rather than try to convince someone who has leverage why they should let go of their preconceived notions. However, once you get the job, the real games begin. To get ahead, you will have to put on different hats, and, more importantly, know when to hide things and reveal them strategically.

Lessons From Monsters #1:

The Curious Case of Chris Watts and the Importance of Non-verbal Communication

The story of Chris Watts is a disturbing tale highlighting the importance of observation and is a good crash course in spotting a liar. To even attempt to start reading more insidious people, it's good to start with a person who did everything wrong.

Chris Watts carries the rare distinction of a murderer who is also a family annihilator. This is an especially rare crime that society finds heinous because it goes against every instinct a father and a husband should have. With a troubled marriage looming, Chris engaged in having an affair with another woman. Instead of divorcing his wife and seeing his children every other weekend, he burned it all to the ground.

In 2018 Watts killed his wife Shannan, his two daughters, Bella and Celeste, and his unborn son, Nico. Watts disposed of the bodies at his job site and thought he was free to live his new life while also getting to play the victim.

Chris Watts did not count on Shannan's observant friend. She had spent the whole weekend with Shannan at a conference and noticed that her friend was distressed the entire time. She knew Shannan would never disappear with the kids, stop answering her phone or miss a doctor's appointment like she had done the morning of the murder.

This friend most likely ruined Watt's plan by calling the cops immediately. The body cam footage hinted at Watt's actions right away. First, when cops told him that his wife was not answering the door and could be unconscious, he did not give the police permission to kick down his door like a normal husband probably would have.

Neighbors noted that Watts was way outside of his baseline. He was usually a quiet man, but he was suddenly very chatty. He was nervous but not frantic. His body language translated into stress, with his arms spread and hands on the back of his head (a position that opens up the lungs to let more air in). He is seen constantly looking at his phone instead of engaging with investigators. This is all still entirely circumstantial since this is a stressful situation, but Watt's behavior started setting off alarms. When he watched camera footage of that night, he averted his gaze from a video that, to the cop, could provide clues into his family's disappearance.

While authorities looked for the missing family, Watts made the inexplicable decision to go on TV and play the distressed father looking for his family. Instead of looking sympathetic, the audience at home thought to themselves, "this guy totally did it." His effect was flat for someone searching heaven and earth for his family. He spoke of wanting his girls back with the same tone as someone who wants their favorite show to be revived by Netflix. His word choices were also suspect. He avoided using names a lot, referring to Bella and Celeste as "those girls," putting distance between him and his crime. He was arrested and later confessed to the whole thing.

Spotting Frauds, Liars, and Other Hurtful People

All this is useful for gauging your friend's emotional state or knowing when to back out of the room when you are getting ready to ask your boss something, but can it protect against truly dangerous people? There is good news and bad news. The good news is that most criminals are not as bright as they think. These people are loud, overconfident, and easy to spot if you know what to look for. Bad news, the intelligent ones will take more than some body language reading.

Abusers that are smart tend to study people, know what works, and know their limitations with that person. They can infiltrate a person's life through many means, one of which is called *mirroring*. This is when a person picks up the mannerisms of another. This is often done subconsciously, but a psychological component can turn this means of survival and turn it into a weapon. We tend to like people that resemble us. A person good at mirroring will let someone take the lead for a while and mirror their tone, mannerisms, and everything to get that person comfortable. When they have that person trapped (say by that person investing in a lot of money or getting someone pregnant), they are free to drop the mask. By that time, the person is so invested that they feel like they have no other option, and the abuser can pick away their self-esteem and trap them further. It is a vicious process; many of us have been or know someone lost to this.

Well, you may be thinking, "all those crime shows and podcasts tell me that these are all psychopaths, and those have to be easy to spot." Unfortunately, that attitude is not only stigmatizing to the neurodivergent but also dangerous to you. You must let go of the notion that bad people are easy to spot because they are "not like you." Let's dispel some myths about the mental illnesses associated with these kinds of people. First, these are all part of Cluster B personality disorders. They include:

- Antisocial Personality Disorder

- Borderline Personality Disorder

- Narcissistic Personality Disorder

- Histrionic Personality Disorder

These are the disorders when we think of when we see criminal masterminds, villains on TV, and sometimes people we flat-out don't like. These people are not born monsters; some theories involve genetics, brain region malformation, and unstable environments. Some go out to do heinous things but most never commit a crime. They can end up as a bank president, in a multilevel marketing scheme, or as an elected politician.

These do not automatically mean that a person is intelligent, wildly capable, or even unstable. It's fair to say some of these exist on a spectrum and any person can exhibit these qualities from time to time. For the most part, these people realize early on that it will not benefit them to commit crimes and end up in jail. Furthermore, not every criminal is diagnosable because they do not meet all the criteria for these disorders.

With intense therapy starting at childhood, and a stable upbringing, you may end up a functional member of society without that, and with opportunity, these traits can lead people down dark paths. There are nine narcissistic traits used for diagnosis. A person who is diagnosable has to exhibit five of these:

1. Having a massive sense of self-importance

2. Need for admiration and validation from others

3. Entitled to special treatment

4. Overstating accomplishments

5. The inability to accept criticism

6. Delusions of grandeur

7. Willingness to exploit others

8. Lack of empathy for others

9. Arrogant behavior or the need to be the center of attention

These traits, coupled with impulsivity, explosive anger, intelligence, charm, and a violent streak can make a person dangerous.

However, these traits can also make someone socially unaware. If they have a blind spot to how their behavior is perceived by others, they cannot manipulate anyone. This level of intelligence is what separates people like Elliot Rogers from someone like Jim Jones.

Lessons From Monsters #2:

Elliot Rogers — The Man Who Had Everything and Yet Had Nothing to Offer

Elliot Rogers was a twenty-two-year-old man who in frustration with being a virgin, went out and murdered six people after writing a manifesto. Those pages detailed an extremely entitled, jealous child. When he was young he would regularly throw tantrums at his rich father and stepmother, and would regularly dump hobbies if he was not good right away. He harbored hated for his mixed Asian heritage. However, the most concerning part was his attitude toward women.

He could not believe that just having rich parents, a BMW, nice clothes, and a lavish lifestyle was not enough to attract girls. He blamed it on the "cruelty of women" and "obnoxious men." What Elliot did not take into account was his wretched personality. Even as an adult he was petulant, impulsive, bitter, and clearly viewed women as objects rather than actual people.

Elliot's misogynistic streak was not a secret; his parents sent him to therapy and tried to get older male figures to give him dating advice. Thanks to his mindset, none of the advice or therapy ever reached Elliot. He instead let his rage fester until he decided to go on a killing spree. He first killed his roommates (all male) because he was jealous that they could get girlfriends. His goal was to go to a sorority house, kill everyone inside and torch it. While in the end, he did manage to kill six people, it was not nearly the badass "mountains of skulls and rivers of blood" he talked about in his manifesto. He eventually crashed his car and when he realized he had been cornered, Elliot turned the gun on himself; immortalizing himself as a joke on the internet.

Thanks to his profound social ineptitude, Elliot Rogers was never able to sink his claws into an unfortunate woman nor was he able to gain real friends. Despite coming from wealth, he was such a blinking neon sign of trouble, no one wanted anything to do with him. He failed to see people other than himself as individuals with their own preferences and motivations. That was his downfall, and this awareness marks the difference between abusers who struggle, chase people away, and only serve to drag people down from the genuinely insidious types that can use our weaknesses to exploit us.

This makes psychology a double-edged sword in our society. There might be someone out there who has abusive traits and can size people up automatically. Knowing what to look out for will at the very least weed out the more pathetic lot before they can infiltrate your life.

What needs to be made clear is that you cannot just scan a person and get their whole life story. Unfortunately because of crime dramas, and body language "experts" that are willing to promise anything to sell books or classes people see it as infallible and almost magical. There are so many extenuating circumstances to a lot of the signs above. What people don't tell you is that you need what is called a *baseline*. This is a person's natural state that you can only get a sense of if you have spent time with them. It's why police ask innocuous questions and part of the reason they are so friendly at the start of an interview.

They need to see you when you are honest to pick out the points where you may lie or feel stressed. For example, bobbing the knee up and down is regarded as a sign of stress. It can be if someone is typically quite still, but if someone has a ton of caffeine or has ADHD, it is almost expected even if they aren't particularly stressed.

Can't I Just Keep Away From the Obvious Bad Guys?

If only it were that easy. Yes, it can be easy to avoid people that are loud about their less than savory traits or cut a person out after they buy a gun when they have no respect for human life. While there is a lot you can look out for in other people, the person you have to start with is yourself. What signs are you giving off, what information are you broadcasting freely, and what kind of traps can you fall into? Human psychology can be quite predictable and if we lack self-awareness we can be taken for a ride by shady businesses, companies running ads, and abusers.

What Have We Learned?

- Words are quite possibly the least reliable pieces of information at your disposal.

- Body language can make or break you. First impressions matter so it's best to be on your toes.

- It is best to relax and let your body channel some of its energy into hand gestures and good posture. Do not overcompensate your way into looking rigid.

- Learn to mirror people's body language to start rapport. Maintain eye contact, and laugh when they do to ingratiate yourself.

- Reading the face can clue you into a person's thought process and can help you spot dishonesty.

- It's not just the words that are spoken, it is how they are spoken that matters. You can have the most reliable information out there, but if you can't deliver it to a crowd in a way that is engaging, no one will care.

- By using body language and nonverbal communication in context you can spot a liar pretty easily.

- You are dealing with two classes of narcissistic personality types, those that broadcast their greatness to the world and crave attention, and those who will be covert and fool their targets for the purposes of power.

- The loud narcissist is not as dangerous unless they are pushed over the edge. For the most part, they are easily avoidable and do not have the social intelligence to manipulate anyone.

SUBLIMINAL INFLUENCE

"Persuasion can go through obstacles that force cannot"

– YUSUF A. LEINGE

Just because you are quietly living your life doesn't mean that you are not broadcasting your desires, vulnerability, and insecurities to those that might want to use them to their advantage. Companies design ads around them, and criminals know how to target them.

The powers that be are not doing this by covertly putting subliminal messages in our favorite songs telling us to buy gold or join the NAVY. They use our psychology to make us insecure and plant ideas and signals in our heads to get us to comply whether it's opening our wallets or opening our hearts.

The Manipulator That Drives the Economy: Ads

In our modern capitalist world, nothing drives the economy quite like advertisements. We like to think of them as annoying, skippable, and ineffective, but they are much cleverer than we give them credit for. They can make us crave food on a physiological level, make us solve problems we did not know existed, and spend money on useless products. They are engineered to separate us from our hard-earned cash by using our own psyche against us.

Advertising Method #1:

Put the Product in the Customer's Hands

The most effective way to convince a person how much they need a product is by letting them experience it for themselves. People love free things, no matter how small and initially uninterested they are in them. This is the best way to turn ambivalence or even doubt into a sale. They can try the product risk-free and they are then given a choice to pay full price. This can be very effective in person because of our first psychological weakness:

We often do irrational things to avoid looking impolite.

If someone successfully gets your attention, you feel trapped because you don't want to look rude by blatantly ignoring them and since you are most likely in a shopping center, you are clearly not up to anything too important.

These salesmen will smile, compliment you, and ask you about your day and the things your product might address. They let the customer hold it or even use it on them all as their sales pitch. This is not just a friendly interaction even though it sure is dressed like one; it is a calculated move to filter out people that their pitch will work on so they can move product. This is even worse when the product in question is a toy that a child can try, get attached to, and start begging for it.

This is not limited to the free samples at Costco, or hair product stands at the mall; this is a huge tactic in the digital age. Free weeks or even months with a product make a person comfortable and even reliant on it.

Netflix was smart enough to give out a free month when people heard about the content they subscribed to; some thought they would get in, watch one show and get out. A lot of those people have now been subscribed for over a decade. It works because the customer thinks they are gaining something when in reality they are being advertised to. Some companies rely on this by banking on people just forgetting to cancel their free trials once they are done. They make the money and don't have the burden of hosting you on a server.

The Dark Side of Trying Products:
The Freemium or Pay to Win Model

This is a tactic that has become increasingly common in games and apps. Sometimes it resembles letting someone try a product, but this tactic has also introduced gambling to adults and children who have never set foot in a casino. In its more innocent mode, it is just letting someone try a worse version of an app or service. It will be slow, missing essential features, and just be riddled with ads. The product is functional for a few tasks but not enough that it is easy or thorough.

After some time, you will exhaust all the free features and realize that your app use has been very surface level the entire time. If you want to upgrade, that will cost you a subscription. Once again, it's a decent sales tactic, but it has taken a twisted turn in the gaming market.

The way video games make money has changed a lot in the last decade and has changed the medium for the worst. It's no longer about releasing an epic story with side quests, great mechanics, and great characters; it's now about sucking as much money out of the player as possible and well beyond the initial purchase of the game. Online games are a haven for this. Every game has some sort of in-game currency to unlock the game's full features faster. Since these games are online with millions of other players, being at a steep disadvantage because you didn't buy *Shark Cards, Gems,* or *Pokecoins.* You might be able to unlock those features, but it takes enough grinding that it becomes unappealing.

Five dollars here and ten dollars there doesn't seem like a big deal at the time. These microtransactions add up, and soon, some people spend hundreds without realizing it.

Kids with an iPad and no adult supervision are notorious for this. Gaming companies know this and use the same design as casinos to get people addicted to slot machines. These games are kind of fun, colorful, bright, and have satisfying noises when you win. The problem is that these games often need boosts to win and get that dopamine hit. Kids will buy virtual diamonds, skins, and advanced weapons or spells for real-world money. Those purchased advantages lead to the thrill of winning and will prompt you to purchase more. In psychological terms, this is known as a *compulsion loop.*

More insidious companies have introduced loot crates into their gaming model. Those kids can get a box filled with random items with just another approval from their parent's credit card. Some boxes can have little value, but if you buy at a higher tier, you might get rare items! Does this sound like gambling–that's because it is.

Slot machines work the same way. That machine associated with a grandma converting her social security checks into quarters is one of the most insidiously engineered devices in existence. They make up 70% of casino revenue, and it's no surprise; it is recognizable and requires no learning curve, with sounds designed to not only be pleasurable but also cut across the ambient noise of a casino. You sit down and push a button that will cause lights and sounds to deliver a dopamine hit that will be compounded if you win.

These wins do not have to be the jackpot; they can be a small reward or a free spin (considered a disguised loss). Your brain will fill with endorphins, and the rush of winning will leave you chasing an even bigger win and an even bigger high. The only problem with that is; that it will rarely, if ever, come. Since you are only putting in a coin at a time, it doesn't feel like a significant loss that a pile of chips does. People will be glued to these for hours. True addicts will insist a machine is "due for a win," becoming violently territorial and even wearing diapers to not lose their machine.

Video game companies have exposed children who are not even allowed to set foot into a casino to the same reward system as gambling addicts are exposed to. Some of these kids are so young they have no concept of money or a credit score; they just know that they can buy the best skins for their Fortnite character or possibly gain an advantage with a loot crate with their parent's credit card number that might even be programmed into the iPad. It became so bad that some countries are looking into legislation to ban loot boxes on children's games.

Advertising Method #2:
Designing Effective Commercials

Not every product is created equally; different strategies are involved in selling luxury goods, everyday items, and pharmaceuticals. It also depends on the target audience, whether it's men, women, old or young. We may think of commercials as annoyances we skip on YouTube or mute on TV, but they are psychologically designed to get the audience to spend money.

The method that everyone is familiar with is casting a celebrity to sell your product. More often than not, stars are good-looking, already have fabulous camera presence, and the audience already likes them. Seeing

Shaquille O'Neil selling *Goldbond* foot powder also makes an otherwise unremarkable product and TV spot memorable without much effort on the production side. Since the audience already has a positive connotation with a celebrity whose work they are a fan of, those feelings of positivity spread to the product. Plus, there is the subject of credibility. Celebrities are rich and have status, traits that we automatically associate with success involving good judgment. The average person is not thinking about the lucrative contract Taylor Swift signed to appear in a Diet Coke ad.

Casting a commercial requires a surprising amount of thought. You would think it would be simple since anybody can swish mouthwash in their mouths and pretend like it's not burning. There is a strategy to cast that once again depends on what is being sold. If it is an everyday product, casting is done based on looking approachable. The director needs the public to see themselves using the product so they can't cast anyone too attractive. Instead, they seek out people that look like an enhanced version of the audience. Clear skin, electric smile, fit (male actors might get away with a dad bod), and, for the most part, young are all mandatory in commercial casting. To feel attached to the product, the audience must see the most idealized version of themselves using it and smiling.

The casting process requires thick skin. Unless the product specifically targets older men, they age out of most castings. Women over thirty age out of most castings and are relegated to yogurt and pharmaceutical ads, and even then, their days are numbered. The exception is ads geared toward older men since aging a man is associated with status and money. Still, these men also have to be pretty fit and handsome to get cast for an ad for erectile dysfunction pills. Ironically even though the men in those ads are portrayed as 50 to 60, the women will never look older than 45 and must be the ideal 45-year-old.

If people like to see themselves, then ads that cast people who are not conventionally attractive would do numbers. After all, it is beneficial to see what the clothes would look like on a model with a higher BMI. You would be wrong. Even if the product is aimed at plus-sized people, the ad will not perform well if the model is more than curvy (higher BMI with an hourglass figure). We cannot be reminded of our flaws lest we associate those negative emotions with the product.

This ideation goes even harder in ads for luxury items. These actors need to be unrelatably good-looking. Suppose they are in a luxury car ad; they also need to sport expensive shoes and watches and be driving down the sunniest road. Luxury brands are seldom depicted inside a home (except for Christmas because people open gifts around the tree) because those who would buy these luxury brands are people on the move. They have money, so they are not sitting at home with that nice watch or bag; they are going out and leading exciting lives.

Fear and Opportunity:
The Advertiser's Bread and Butter

Since we cannot touch, try or smell the product businesses want us to buy, advertisers have to entice the customer in creative ways. The way they do this is by playing on our insecurities and offering a way out. For example, mouthwash companies like *Listerine* made an entire society paranoid that their breath smelled unpleasant, but people were too polite to tell each other. That is how they were able to pivot their floor cleaner into another revenue source as a mouthwash. Razor companies saw an untapped market in women. In the past, western women did not worry about being clean-shaven below the eyebrows. That all changed when ads were released making women self-conscious about body hair. It not only sold an enormous amount of more expensive razors, but it changed the beauty standard associated with women that still persists to this day.

Next time you look at an ad, see what button it's trying to press. There are quite a few that can overlap with a bunch of products:

- Fear of being unhygienic or smelly
- Fear of hair being unkempt
    - If you are a woman, fear that your hair is dull or damaged
- Fear of looking dated or frumpy with clothing
- Fear that your house is dirty
- Fear that your diet is not up to par
- Fear that you are not skinny or muscular enough
- Fear that you might be sick
- Fear that you might be spending too much money (or fear of poverty)

One more fear and opportunity has nothing to do with the product, and that is the fear of missing out or FOMO. You can miss out on saving money, or you can miss out on the product or event itself. That pressure will cause you to act more impulsively. Sales are the most straightforward example of this. We associate holidays like labor day with a day off and one-day sales that may trick us into buying more. Online websites may have a timer counting down when the sale will end, adding a sense of urgency to make a purchase.

Some websites will even artificially inflate the price to make it seem like the lower price is a deal that won't last long when it is just the regular price. This creation of urgency is so pervasive it was made illegal in the European Union and Australia.

Collectors' items are also a version of FOMO. While collecting is not everyone's cup of tea, if there is a market for it, someone will collect it. Some people consider their *Star Wars* action figure and lightsaber collection a hobby. They buy up every version of their favorite characters and put them on display for the world to see. It's a harmless enough source of pride. Then there are the collectors that are in dire need of completing a set. When *Inspector Gadget* came to theaters in 1999 McDonald's played into the FOMO predilection in children. Their happy meals contained parts of Inspector Gadget that all had different functions. The leg was a flashlight; one arm could pick up French fries, another was a water gun, etc. In the end, you got a large Inspector Gadget toy. It was brilliant marketing, and kids all over the country got their parents to take them to McDonald's multiple times to get to the entire figure.

Some collectors feel like a complete collection will have some value in the future. We all remember and rightfully mock the Beanie Baby collectors of the 1990s. With only the power of hype and no empirical evidence, the public at large was convinced that just having a large number of these stuffed bears with their tags intact was a valuable investment. As they buy more or find a bear they have never seen, people forget one thing: they are only valuable if the item is rare. Only a tiny handful of Beanie Babies would net a person some money if they sold them on eBay, but most of them would end up abandoned in attics or sold for cents at garage sales.

Some collector's items have a lot of resale value and are hidden amongst more common items. This is most common in cards. In the past, it was primarily sports cards that caught people's attention, and valuable cards are still sold at auction today. However, lately, game cards are the most significant purchases. Some people legitimately have a passion for, say, Yu-Gi-Oh or Magic the Gathering and will buy decks of cards to find cards that will give them an edge in the game. Others, though, will buy piles and piles of cards they will never play with on the hunt for value. It is the loot crate phenomenon all over only without sounds and lights; just the dopamine hit of opening a new deck. The anticipation alone will release dopamine and serotonin before you even know if the purchase was worth it or not. There is a massive audience for this online where creators will buy hundreds or even thousands of packs of cards at once and open them live so an audience of millions of kids. They can feel the anticipation dopamine rush with the creator; thus, the creator can get their audience addicted to watching their videos live.

Lessons From Monsters #3:

Expectations vs. Reality — Fyre Fest

There is no better lesson about people taking advantage of FOMO than Billy McFarland and the Fyre Fest debacle. Fyre Fest was one of the most successful advertising campaigns in history. The campaign had luxury, status, and mystery all rolled into one. The plan was to have a luxury music festival held in the Bahamas.

There would be 5-star accommodations, top-tier musical guests, food, and alcohol all included in the price of purchase. Before the official commercial, Billy McFarland paid influencers hundreds of thousands each to simply post an orange tile on their social media accounts. This created an air of mystery and anticipation for millions of followers. Everyone wanted to know what this orange tile meant and why their favorite influencers were all posting it. Then the trailer for the event was released.

It looked like an event like no other, models, boats, shots, beaches, swimming pigs to play with; everything to make for a memorable experience. The impression that people got was that they would be hanging out on a beautiful beach with beautiful people where they could share this experience on social media for all to see. Tickets sold out immediately. What they actually purchased was a nightmare.

What people did not know was that when that ad was released, nothing was actually planned despite the date being months away. The island was not reserved and Billy had no choice but to use the outskirts of a Sandals resort. There was no existing infrastructure so logistics were a nightmare. There was no plumbing, no villas, and not even a decent foundation. Billy hired locals (all working with the promise of being paid when the project was done) to set up surplus tents and porta potties for guests.

They were constantly blowing their budget and Billy would charm his way into getting more investor money to buy time. Still, it was never going to be enough and they had to break so many promises. Villas turned into tents, gourmet meals turned into ham sandwiches, and the luxury private plane turned into the equivalent of a *Spirit Airlines* plane with a logo painted on it.

They could not delay the event because of all the loans Billy had taken out. He tried everything to get more money including promising super high-tier packages available for hundreds of thousands of dollars and offering *Fyre bands*. Ticket holders were urged to load money into these bands because the event would be cashless. It was just another way to collect more capital. He owed everyone money in an effort to keep the festival alive because that was his only hope of paying it all back. The day of the festival arrived and the ones that had their flights canceled were the lucky ones.

Those that arrived were met with something more akin to a refugee camp than a music festival. All the acts saw the writing on the wall when they were never paid and pulled out. The fantasy that the Fyre Fest commercial created was replaced with a dangerous nightmare that the guests were now trapped in. They had no recourse since many didn't have cash after loading it all into the Fyre Band.

All other hotels were booked months prior because Billy had the bright idea of holding the festival on the same weekend as a big local festival. All the staff could do was appease the guests with alcohol. They were all trapped and had no choice but to sleep in the tents on the beach.

It was a miracle no one was hurt. The staff were not equipped to deal with hundreds of pissed-off drunk adults and luckily they didn't have to. Any number of things could have happened that would make this story a tragedy instead of kind of funny. People could have drowned, been attacked, gotten lost, hurt, or even killed. The attendees, staff, and locals that put their sweat and blood into trying to fulfill promises were all abandoned by Billy.

In the end, Billy was sent to prison and the company has since been dissolved. What people are left with is a textbook example of a successful advertising campaign that pulled on the desires and fears of the typical millennial and a lesson in making promises you can't keep.

Fear, Opportunity, and Guilt: The Grifters Triad

Using fear and opportunity is an accepted advertising method but when you see that someone is trying to guilt you into spending money or time–that is when your ears should really perk up. Guilt is a powerful motivator. It is not that you will miss out on something; it's that you or your family's lives may be worse without this thing or that you owe someone your energy.

This goes beyond sales though some companies use this strategy. Companies use this when they prompt us to donate to charity. There is the fear the cashier will think we are cheap, the opportunity to rack up some good karma, and guilt in saying no to the child's picture representing the charity. Even though these companies make billions every year, they put the onerous to donate on the average customer while being able to write off the donation on their taxes.

This is a favorite technique of televangelists that prey on fears of hell, disease, and loneliness. They foster a community and preach the word of God all while asking for donations or tithing.

They promise that the power of God's blessing is directly correlated to the amount they donate. These blessings can include wealth, happiness, and most insidious – health. They con desperate people into believing that if they prayed and donated to that exact congregation that their cancer would disappear. It does not help that these televangelists are loud, and passionate, and share "stories" of people whose tumors disappeared after they believed hard enough. These people are so hopeful they are blind to the transparent greed of these "men of God."

They fly in private jets and live in mansions that are the furthest from Christ-like as one could get. People are afraid of dying and what comes after, they have the opportunity for salvation both physical and spiritual and they are injected with religious guilt since doubting a pastor is akin to doubting God.

Learn to Sell Anything Using Techniques From the Masters

Up until now, you have probably been getting frustrated as you realized how often the big business has taken you for a ride. You may hate being a "salesman," but you will have to sell something eventually, whether it's something for work or yourself. These techniques are prevalent because they work and you can make it work for you too.

First impressions are a must and you have to master this before your pitch. Mirroring is quite possibly the most powerful psychological tool at your disposal. It is an easy way to establish rapport and get someone to trust you very quickly. Best of all it is a two-way street because the other person may end up mirroring you unconsciously.

- Square off with them, never stand at an angle, and get close (but not too close). You will have their undivided attention and standing directly face to face instead of at an angle will inspire trust.

- Look at their demeanor: are they shy or more extroverted? A person who is more reserved will probably not appreciate a person who is overbearing and a confident, brash extrovert may find a shy salesman unconvincing. Match the volume of their voice but be confident in what you are selling and why it would be a worthy purchase.

- Give them your undivided attention as well, and try to avoid writing things down as they talk even if it's well-intentioned.

- The exception is your hands, never hide them even if the customer does. Keep your hands out and moving (humans tend to respond better to hand gesticulation) never keep them behind you or in your pockets. Look at advertisements and speeches; the hands are always moving.

- Repetition can be the key to a sale. Say you want to show off an expensive item but the customer is uncertain. You gently go back to it and the benefits when you can. You insert that idea in their head and as you repeat it, you can potentially get the customer invested in the idea of something new and flashy. They start picturing themselves with this car driving down the interstate with the top down or all the compliments they will get from the new couch and the years of joy each item will bring.

- Repeat certain things back to them. If they are ordering something, say the order back to them, not only does it avoid mistakes but the customer feels heard and appreciates that. If they have a specific word choice or phrasing like the way they greet (if they say "good morning" don't respond with "hi") and if they explain what issue they may want to solve by purchasing the product or reveal details about their personal life, reiterate the issue before making the pitch.

The customer sees a bit of a pleasant version of themselves at this point and their trust in you is growing as you build the rapport. Now it's time to actually sell, some of these techniques may sound strange but they are used so much because they work.

- Never use the word "I" this sale is not about you and if the customer is not interested in what you think or your experiences, keep the pitch on how the product will directly benefit them.

- Hit them where it hurts! Play on their fears after all if they are interested in buying something it's because there is a problem they want to solve or something they want to gain. Play up the consequences of what they would lose out on if they don't buy your product.

- Once they are reminded of their insecurities, pitch the product and how it will directly benefit them. They have to leave the conversation wanting the product and the benefits they can gain from it.

- Avoid words like "maybe," "hope," and "honestly." These are filler words that do nothing but inspire doubt. Do not tell an obvious lie but make the sale like you believe in the product.

Here is an exercise: if you are selling something put yourself in your customer's shoes. Let's say you are selling a personal training service and you have a customer on the fence about it. Why would a customer buy into that rather than a regular, cheaper gym membership? Look at their fears:

- They have already failed at getting in shape and they might fail again

- They have already wasted money on previous memberships

- Their health and mobility is getting worse as they age

- They are afraid they will look stupid setting foot in a gym

- They are overwhelmed and don't know where to start

You have to convince them that their fears are founded and that your service will help. If they have fears don't talk them out of it...validate them! The customer will feel heard. For example:

- *I can't seem to keep going to the gym after a month.*

Instead of:

- *Don't be so hard on yourself. We all have lives and you should keep trying.*

A better follow-up would be:

- *It's difficult to make it to the gym without accountability, life gets in the way and it's a waste of money. Luckily, our clients keep to their schedules because they love our trainers.*

The "kind" thing would be to tell a person not to be so hard on themselves, but you might have talked yourself out of a sale because you did not convince them they need the service. You did the opposite.

What Have We Learned?

- You can learn a lot about how people think, and how to make them do what you want from ads.

- Admiration is transferable from person to object.

- We like to see an idealized version of ourselves and are more apt to trust that person when they recommend something.

- Businesses will play on our fears to make us see an opportunity, but the worst ones will also use guilt.

- Mind games that play on scarcity and mystery can compel a person to act out of just wanting to be in the know.

THE ART OF DARK PERSUASION

"If you would persuade, you must appeal to interest rather than intellect"

– BENJAMIN FRANKLIN

So far, the examples of how our own psychology can be turned against us have been mostly light-hearted. However, there are people out there that can use our natural thought patterns to do more harm than a higher credit card bill.

It is essential to recognize when and how a person can screw us over financially, abuse us emotionally or harm us physically. Staying vigilant and potentially turning the tide will help keep you safe from people that only serve to do you harm. However, we can also take these lessons and use them to make us more persuasive and effective.

Reprogramming Yourself

Before you go out into the world and try to use body language and sales pitches to get what you want, the first person you have to manipulate is yourself. If you do not believe in yourself and what you are saying and show that when interacting with people, you will look like a liar no matter how truthful you are. You might have some serious self-doubts, illogical fears, and fears that have been justified by bad experiences. As much as you try to hide it, if you do not have mastery over your own head, you will never have mastery over anyone else.

Time for a bit of tough love: why should anyone believe in you, follow you, trust you or even listen to you if you are projecting doubt? People follow those who they see as powerful, intelligent, and charismatic. If you mumble your way through life, slouching, with your hands in your pockets you will never climb up any ladder. In this world that takes social intelligence and no matter how right you may be if your delivery is wrong people will go with a huckster because their message is in a prettier package.

It will take work, practice, and an intense level of self-awareness but with some techniques and changes in your way of thinking you will be able to convince yourself you can rise to the top. These techniques are dressed up in different ways, cognitive behavioral therapy, Neurolinguistic Programming (NLP), magical thinking, and manifestation. They all have their own levels of credibility ranging from accepted to complete quackery depending on if the person administering it is a professional genuinely trying to help fix issues or a "life coach" that is trying to teach other life coaches. There is a surprising amount of overlap with some of their core tenants mainly because humans are all motivated by a few key things. Once that is accomplished you will be able to convince others.

Visualize Your Goals and What Person You Want to Be

This sounds silly but visualization is a great way to get you to focus on becoming a better you. It is not just looking up at the ceiling and imagining yourself in a mansion with a gold toilet, a stack of cash, and models on each arm. In NLP this is the key to setting yourself up for success. You get an idea of what you want and you play it in your head. Whether it's breaking a bad habit or hitting a certain milestone, the act of not only thinking about it by picturing it in our mind will program and motivate us to seek it out.

This concept is taken a step further in cognitive behavioral therapy. Say you have a task you have been procrastinating on, a project, an assignment, paying bills, etc. If you have an anxiety problem when you think visualizing you think of the consequences or pitfalls:

- *The project will look bad*

- *I failed and I feel stupid for even trying*

- *I will have my lights shut off because I keep procrastinating*

- *I will fail the class and then fail out of school*

This is a psychological phenomenon known as the *Fortune Teller* effect and taken further it can become *Catastrophizing*. These are cognitive distortions we have all fallen victim to at some point or maybe even all the time. To counteract this you can try some positive visualization before you set out to do what you want.

Say you want to run a 5K race. Before your mind pirouettes about how you will never be able to run that far, how sweaty and hot you will be, and how sore you will be the next day from practice try this type of visualization.

- Picture the weather on the day of the race, maybe it will be sunny with a nice breeze, will the air be crisp? Just hold that image in your mind.

- When you run the race, think of the cheers in the crowd, smiling and waving at all your friends, you are keeping up with everyone and your time is good, you are proud in that moment.

- Now the most important part is to think about when you finish the race. How will the air smell? How will that first drink of water feel? Who will be there to congratulate you? Will it be your family, maybe a friend, maybe your fellow racers? How will you feel? You will be proud because all your hard work has paid off, you are beaming because your loved ones are proud, and you will get a hit of dopamine when you post pictures of you finishing the run on your social media. Most of all you are proud because you proved to yourself that you could do this. You did not let those negative thoughts stop you and you know you can take on a more difficult challenge.

Other things you can add are positive affirmations about what you want:

- *I am stronger than I was yesterday*

- *I am confident and no one can take that away from me*

- *No matter what I will be okay (*put a pin in this one we'll come back to it*)*

Do these feel a bit silly, yeah, but they can help. Your thoughts, goals, and fears all swirl in your head like a nebulous force of electricity in your brain. They are fleeting, hypothetical, and difficult to call on when you need them. Think of it like those game shows where someone is locked in a wind chamber and has to grab money or a certain prize before time runs out. In the heat of the moment, it is very difficult to swipe what you need out of the air.

By speaking to a therapist if you have one, confiding in another person, or writing down or speaking an affirmation you organize and breathe life into your problems. When they are real you can put some valid perspective on things instead of worrying about everything. Same as the visualization exercise. You have a goal in mind but your thoughts are so jumbled by your doubts that the good thoughts get lost in the mix and those are the ones that will motivate you.

This is also similar to the *Swish Technique* in NLP. This is meant to break a habit by visualizing yourself as a better, more fulfilled person by not indulging the habit. It is helped by a swish sound or visual to help with the shift in mind frame. If a person is an alcoholic and they suddenly feel like drinking, they can picture themselves happy and sober with their children. Our brains can be powerful motivators on their own; you just need to know when to call it out.

70

Model Yourself After the Experts and PRACTICE

It's sometimes not enough to practice. What might reinforce the behavior is copying the masters. You want to be able to give a speech, watch, listen then recite the address down to the pauses and hand movements.

Watch politicians, Ted Talks, and trailblazing figures deliver their ideas and pay attention to the reaction. You want to be more confident and act like your favorite celebrity or character (remember to reinforce their positive attributes, not the flaws that make for good TV).

Look at how they walk, their mannerisms, how they answer questions and their core beliefs. What about them makes you like them or at least pay attention? Do you want to be a confident businessman like Don Draper from *Mad Men,* then embody him. Suppose you want to be a leader, look at characters like Captain America. With enough time, what you are missing will become clear. Once you understand what being this person is all about, you can start adjusting the mannerisms to tailor them to your life. After all, if you want to be like Doctor House to become a better medical provider, maybe stick to the out-of-the-box thinking and focus and less to the terrible bedside manner.

Learn to Face Your Fears: Convince Yourself That Everything Will Be Alright

This is the basis of a lot of therapy that involves anxiety. Thanks to our cognitive distortions we can only see the worst in a situation. As a result, we put off a task or abandon it together. It does not even have to be a physical or financial risk, a blow to someone's pride is an unconscious but a giant risk. Have you ever committed yourself to starting a cool but expensive hobby like photography or oil painting? You buy all the stuff you need to start then you either get ready to practice and chicken out or abandon the whole thing after one attempt. The result is a small store's worth of abandoned kits and dreams.

Next time you start to feel nervous about starting something new, ask yourself:

- *What exactly am I afraid of?*

- *What proof do I have of the validity of these fears?*

- *What is the worst that can happen?*

- *How realistic is that worst-case scenario?*

- *What if something really good happens? How will you feel?*

- *What will be the most likely outcome if you push forward with your plan?*

- *What will be the most realistic outcome of this endeavor?*

- *Is this realistic outcome that bad?*

You will put a lot of things into perspective. In reality, getting out of our comfort zones and even failing a bit is good. We are terrified of failure as adults because it can land us on the unemployment line or in divorce court. Realistically everyday failures that keep us from specific goals are entirely innocuous. If your oil painting comes out bad, you can try again. The painting gods will not come down; cut off your hands and light your canvas on fire. You just have a crappy painting now.

If you approach someone who is not interested at a bar, you never see that person again. If you apply for a job and you don't get it, just apply for another one. Some decisions have weight, but we must separate actual consequences from blows to pride or inconsequential failures. As you fail, you realize that your life is still the same as before you tried the thing. You might have a little less money in your bank account, but you tried and learned.

In cognitive behavioral therapy, there is a technique known as *grounding* when you start to feel anxious in the present moment. All those worst-case scenarios run through your head, making you physically sick. In grounding, you stop the panic in its tracks by focusing on the current environment. You feel your body in space, your feet on the floor, and breathe in and out. You realize you are safe in your current environment. The brain is fantastic, but it cannot distinguish everyday stress from having to give a presentation from when a pack of wolves chased down our ancestors. It just knows it is in danger and prepares for fight or flight. Once you are grounded, go through those sets of questions to cement that it's going to be okay.

Becoming comfortable with failure will open the door to success because you won't be afraid to start. You set small accomplishable goals. Instead of "write a book," try brainstorming different book ideas and come up with a list. Then you can research topics and find the topic you gravitate to the most. Then outline the book, get all your research together, and go chapter by chapter. If it turns out you don't like doing complex research on a topic, switch to a new topic, or don't like how a particular chapter is going, retool it. Lofty goals are unspecific, with many sub-steps that are way more work than you realize. Those small victories will fuel you, and they will carry you on over to the next task.

You will start succeeding, and that earned confidence spills over into other things. Maybe you walk a little straighter; you are less afraid to share an idea at work.

You may want to take on other things that keep you from being the person you want to be. Some fears can be taken care of by exposing ourselves to them and their outcomes. For example, volunteering to give a small presentation at work and realizing that the floor did not swallow you and you knew how to sidestep a few difficult questions. You realized you could talk to a crowd and responded well under pressure. Maybe you will try a more complicated topic with a bigger audience next time.

Successful Reprogramming Keeps You Safe

Once you have broken a few bad habits, you may start to stand taller and speak with more conviction. You just sound more intelligent and more self-assured. People looking to take advantage of others tend to avoid people that look confident because there is not much they can offer you. There is no room for leverage or any visible weakness to exploit. Since you are not slouching, they have no reason to probe for information by asking, "what's wrong?" This will not only keep you safe, but it will keep the people you surround yourself with safe as well. There are always more vulnerable people to go after and ruin.

Lessons From Monsters #4:

Jim Jones

If you want a lesson in manipulating not only the fears and flaws but the egos of a group of people, there is no more horrifying teacher than Jim Jones. Contrary to the narrative, the Jonestown massacre was not a mass suicide of a bunch of evangelical loons that were hypnotized by a crazy man with a sick pair of sunglasses. Rather this event was a study about how one man turned a group of once normal people into monsters who he would eventually murder.

Lesson 1: He Had Something to Offer

No one would have followed Jim Jones if he was not tangibly effective. Had he not become (or the better phrase, revealed himself to be) a megalomaniacal cult leader, people would remember him fondly in the civil rights movement. You see, Jim Jones was key to desegregating many towns in Indiana. He helped the African American community get electricity and provided a voice to a group that otherwise would have no recourse. He did an unquestionable amount of good in that community.

This following evolved into *The People's Temple.* This cult disguised as a congregation preached socialist ideals and built a paradise where everyone would be equal. This was an enticing message for a lot of people who were cast out by society or were sick of the United States government and capitalism. Towards the end, as *The People's Temple* fell into squalor, one of the things that kept people going was remembering the good times. There used to be singing, dancing, and a sense of community in Jonestown. They even had a chimpanzee mascot called Mr. Muggs. Many held out hope that if they could just make Jim Jones happy, they could get their paradise back. Until the last day, the upper ring promised to improve things, and people believed them.

Lesson 2: He Had Watched People His Entire Life

Jim Jones did not get people to Guyana by raving he was Jesus. Jim Jones was dangerous because he was smart and systematically studied people for years. He saw how the town regarded his meek father—as a joke. Jones resolved to have influence and power over people and was willing to work for it. He spent his school days bossing around the boys in his class before they got sick of him. Instead of realizing he was abrasive and demanding, he found new targets, sorry friends. He went after the younger children who followed him without hesitation. They played his games, and Jones wanted to see how far he could push them. At one point, he took the kids on a late-night field trip to a casket workshop and tested his control over the boys by making them lay in the caskets.

In his adulthood, he would take on a job as an orderly at a nursing home. There he learned to get the elderly to like him. Apparently, he was a joy to be around and made the residents feel comfortable. This seems like a lighthearted time in Jim Jones' life, but it is darker when you realize that many of the Jonestown residents were elderly.

The elderly are among the most vulnerable populations despite the notion that wisdom comes with age. The reality is that they can be manipulated due to their loneliness, failing health, and inexperience with the modern world. Jim knew how to push the right buttons and not only got people to like him but trust him.

Lesson 3: He Was a Magician at Convincing People He Was a Great Man

Jim Jones had to convince people that he was different but also the real deal. On top of his socialist rhetoric, there was also his reputation as a healer. He would take people from the audience, guess their ailments, and claim to cure them. Some were plants, but others thought they were being cured of cancer and other diseases. The magic trick was that he would have spies in the audience, mingle in the crowd, and recall specific complaints from specific people (told you he was brilliant). He then called them on stage and pretended to heal them.

Sometimes all he needed was crowd psychology; he excited a group with speeches, calls to action, and injustices, and the energy in the room was palpable. When a person is singled out and called up, they are nervous but are also feeding off the crowd's excitement. The adrenaline and the placebo effect are powerful, and they will temporarily feel better. To add an extra sprinkle, he would sometimes have a nurse slip chicken guts into a person's mouth, so when they inevitably spit it out, the crowd would think it was the tumor. The "healed" person fed on the crowd's distraction so much that they left feeling like a miracle had happened to them.

Jim Jones was so confident in his delivery, magic tricks, and understanding of people that no one had any choice but to deny him. His word was intoxicating, men followed him, and some women even wanted the honor of sleeping with a god walking on earth.

Lesson 4: He Never Let Anyone Forget He Was in Charge

People who seek power for the wrong reasons are often very protective of it. They would be publicly humiliated if anyone challenged him or broke the rules. Early on, this just involved getting yelled at in front of the congregation and sometimes by the assembly. Still, he knew to end the punishment by hugging them and telling the perpetrator they were forgiven and that the punishment was for their own good.

As the People's Temple evolved, however, punishments became more severe. First, people were spanked with a paddle, then beaten with a rubber hose. The penalties were now entertainment for a crowd that needed someone's misfortune for catharsis. There was even a point where Jim Jones forced elderly rule breakers to get into boxing matches (yes, this is real) with teenagers. They would be forced to fight until they lost.

As his grip continued to slip, he would take the most problematic people and essentially drug them into submission. This also included women who refused his sexual advances.

Lesson 5: He Knew Which Egos to Indulge

Jim Jones had a problem with his demographics. While most of his early members were disenfranchised and had no access to education, as the People's Temple expanded, he was getting more college-educated yuppies.

These people knew when Jones was wrong about politics and current events. Once again, he would publicly humiliate them in front of the congregation. This time Jones would take them aside and tell them that he appreciated their criticism. Jones played to their egos, telling them they were insightful. Still, their tact was off justifying his misinformation by telling the skeptics that the congregation was made up of "simple" people, but they needed the message. Jones realized they were in a position of power, and he had to reign that in.

He would bring them into his inner circle and give them jobs with responsibility. He kept potential enemies incredibly close and turned who he could into allies.

Lesson 6: He Isolated His People, Forcing Them to Depend on Him

When Jim Jones felt he had a sufficient hold on his people, he isolated them in different compounds. He eventually got a group of over 900 people to move to Guyana. Not only that but before joining, everyone had to sign over every asset they had to the congregation. After all, this was a socialist extremist group and having any possessions clashed with that. However, it was an insidious trap. People often ask, "why didn't these people leave?" The answer is simple;

they couldn't. The church gave them a job, a community, and a purpose at the expense of their material possessions. This means they had no money to leave and no job to feed themselves or their families.

When people join these groups, they tend to burn bridges on the way out of their old life, and Jones knew that. To maintain that illusion, mail would be intercepted so members would have no idea they would be welcomed home with open arms. The members just knew they were sending out letters, and no one was returning them if they were reaching out even a little. Even though years of drug abuse (it takes a lot of amphetamines and quaaludes to run a cult and get beauty sleep) exposed the fact that Jones was no longer the benevolent figure he once was, everyone was trapped. Jim Jones and the People's Temple was the only place left to the members.

The people were physically isolated, surrounded by others who believed in the message. Even if they could return home, there was another fundamental human weakness that got in the way:

- *We cannot accept it when we are wrong.*

Being proven wrong in general is a severe blow to our self-esteem. We could be wrong about silly things, and while some people can put their hands up and admit to a mistake, many choose to double down. This is not your average disagreement on whether tomatoes are a fruit or a vegetable; people staked their identities on this, invested everything, and preached the good word of Jim Jones to everyone they knew. They not only trusted this man, but they were also willing to follow him to hell on earth. The people you put faith in are a reflection of you, your judgment, and your values. A temple member must realize they were wrong about everything and come crawling back. This shame is so powerful it keeps people tied to Jim Jones for the rest of their lives.

Lesson 7: He Exhausted Them

Exhaustion is one of the most powerful tools in an abuser's arsenal. Tired people are irrational, bendable, desperate, and need to cling to something. He used his power over his group to hold them in mass, forcing them to stand for hours, sometimes well into the night, to listen to him rant. He would have the loudspeakers play his messages all day with no breaks, and when he got tired of talking, the congregation was in luck; the notes were also on tape!

While there was a sense of love and community in the People's Temple, there was always an aura of mistrust because everyone snitched on everyone else. The inciting incident leading to the massacre came when a trained child shouted to the congregation that a note was passed to an outsider. The temple was your friend, but you could never be honest with the individuals in the temple, or they might take your grievances to the upper echelon. In the best-case scenario, you are screamed at in front of everyone, and hopefully, you won't be put in a boxing ring with someone way stronger than you. Jim Jones had one other means of exhausting his flock, and it led them to their doom.

Lesson 8: He Gave Them an Enemy

Part of what made Jim Jones feel so important was his persecution complex. He not only wanted his people to worry about him and their slice of heaven, but he also wanted to feel important enough to have enemies in the government. He would stage assassination attempts early on and even faked his death and resurrection. He would lecture them for hours about how the government would bust down the door one day, torture all the children, and burn it all to the ground. The congregation heard this repeatedly, and with the information coming into Jonestown being tightly monitored, no one knew otherwise.

The truth is that while Jim Jones was being watched, he was not exactly Malcolm X on the scale of government surveillance. The government was interested in him for more bureaucratic matters like the post office having to get Social Security checks over to the residents and the ethics of using their HAM radio for something other than recreation.

This did not stop Jim Jones from revving up the paranoia. Every staged assassination or "story" about how the government was out to get them only emboldened this weary group. He knew how to whip his crowd up in a frenzy just like a man he admired for his oration skills–Adolf Hitler. He needed to see how far he could push his followers.

On several occasions, Jim Jones would call either his upper echelon or the entire congregation to the temple in the middle of the night. He talked about how the mission was over, and the government was ready to torture them. He then had cups of juice (sometimes wine for the top members) and told them it was time to die and drink. These were known as White Nights. The mass poisoning did not come out of nowhere, it was practiced, and Jim Jones knew it would work.

Lesson 9: The Narcissist's Fatal Flaw

When dealing with a true narcissist, they have a major flaw. They cannot accept failure or criticism and would burn everything to the ground rather than admit to being flawed. This can make them extremely dangerous if they view you as a possession slipping away from them, so it is essential to recognize the signs early. Jim Jones is a sobering lesson of someone who could not accept an ounce of rejection.

A visit from congressman Leo Ryan precipitated the last days of Jonestown. He went to some constituents' behest to ensure their family members' safety. To his surprise, they let him in for a visit. Everyone put their best foot forward, and Leo Ryan had enough assurance from the tour that everything was alright and told the congregation as much. Still, about 30 people wanted to defect; some made a run for the jungle, and others wanted the congressman to ship them out. This put Jim Jones into a tailspin. He should have been happy with the outcome, the government would leave them alone, and only 3% of his followers escaped when they had a chance. The upper echelon was relieved at first because they could get on with business as usual, but Jim Jones put a stop to that.

In classic narcissist fashion, Jim Jones could not accept that anyone would dare leave him. Between the dilapidated conditions of the compound, his drug abuse, and the abandonment of a handful of people, Jim Jones decided that it was over, and he was going to take everyone with him. Some have dubbed this an extended suicide. When a person decides that they want to die and because he sees another person (most often their child) as an extension of themselves, he decides to have that person follow him. He backed everyone into a corner when he had the congressman killed and told everyone it was time for the last White Night.

He loaded up Flavor Aid buckets with cyanide and told everyone it was time. On the tape, he rushes people to get their kids ready for death. With the children gone, the parents would have nothing else to live for, so most of them drank their poison willingly. As children screamed, convulsed, and foamed at the mouth Jim Jones told one final lie: that it would not be painful, and the children were just crying because it tasted bitter. Some resisted, and they were forcibly injected with the poison by their fellow members.

Of course, a narcissist like Jim Jones was not about to go out screaming and gurgling; he had someone else shoot him in the back of the head. History would not remember him as a great man. His only contribution to society is the occasional quote "don't drink the Kool-Aid," which is not even accurate, as well as a lesson in how anyone could fall under a narcissist's spell and be taken down with them.

Recognizing the Abuser's Playbook

Now, what was the point of that story? You are probably not in a cult headed for ruin in the jungle so how does this apply to you? Abuse comes in all shapes and sizes. There is physical, emotional, sexual, and financial among others that only people with the darkest imaginations can come up with.

Abusers can come in two flavors. There are those with power (physical, social, financial) who know they can break a target without much effort. There are also those who slither into a person's life while wearing the mask of a good person; they form bonds and as time passes they slowly reveal who they are. Both of these are extremely dangerous to anyone. Abusers and criminals tend to adhere to techniques that help them pick out, and hurt others all for their own personal gain. By knowing the things that you are doing and how someone who has picked you out as a target might interact with you, there might be some ways you can protect yourself.

Knowing When You Are in Bed With a Deceiver

It takes a lot to realize someone is manipulating you. You are confronted with an error in your judgment, blindness, and potentially your whole world crashing down. You will have to sit down and take stock of your relationships. It is okay that this is difficult and even embarrassing.

Trust is a funny thing. Many people see it as a binary issue; either you trust someone, or you don't. It is a lot more complicated than that. You trust people on a spectrum, which is relatively easy to obtain under the right circumstances. For example, you trust the waiter at the restaurant you are patronizing for the first time to walk away with your credit card and not take down the information. You trust an Uber driver you have never met not to murder you and stuff you in a suitcase. However, you most likely would not trust an Uber driver enough to let them into your house.

Trust can quickly be gained, and with enough interaction, it will grow. Still, it can be easily broken if it is still premature. If you say the wrong thing on a first date, you will most likely not be invited on a second date because that trust was broken. It is why first impressions are so important. It is how that person will see you for a long time; if it is a bad one, the other person will hold that against you. If you are the new guy and make a weird joke to the wrong person, it will color their perception of you and your work unless you make a serious effort to fix it. Two ingredients, though, will make soft trust into rock-hard cement; love and investment.

People and businesses looking to take advantage of others know this well, thanks to another fundamental human weakness:

- *The sunk cost fallacy*

If someone has invested emotional energy, love, or money into a person, the idea that that person would turn around and deceive them is unfathomable. It can be considered the ultimate judge of character, and you have failed. Still, you remember the good times or promises made, and you think if I stick with this, I will get something out of it. If I give up now, I will lose everything. You will always have something more to lose, whether it's time, energy, money, dignity, or even your life. Remember, the best time to plant a tree was twenty years ago; the second best time to plant one is right now. If this is a person you are dealing with, look for patterns and signs and examine them

Love Bombing

This is an insidious start to any relationship. A person gets your trust very quickly by being on their best behavior and showering you with love and attention. They may start using very personal pet names, invite you to move in, give you lavish gifts and introduce you to their family immediately.

This honeymoon googly-eyed phase of any relationship is where a person is most vulnerable. It is new and exciting, and a person can feed that excitement with a lot of validation and material possessions. The problem is that it is not real, nor is it sustainable. Slowly but surely, things slow down, the gifts stop, the praise stops, and they might start becoming passive-aggressive and negging you. But you turn a blind eye to it because there were good times to cling to, and that trust was cultivated very quickly. You will chase a fantasy of that person, and they will continue to trap you.

Eroding Your Self Esteem

People often think of abusive relationships as only having physical and sexual violence in them. A lot of abuse can start and continue to be emotional. So this person you have moved in with very quickly has now started to change a bit. They have begun criticizing you for small things like the way you dress or your hairstyle. It is passive-aggressive and kind of annoying, but if you look past it, maybe appearances are very important to them. But then they start demeaning your friends; you try to laugh it off and will just keep them apart. Finally, they start really coming down on you, calling you stupid, ugly, unlovable, and selfish. It is repeated by someone you love and trust so much that you start to believe it. No matter what you do, the insults continue, and other phrases peppered in are:

- *No one other than me will love you*
- *No wonder your ex left you*
- *I could find someone so much better than you*

- *I am wasting my time and money on you*

This person has destroyed your confidence but is not letting you go. Instead, they are pulling you in tighter because they know that you are starting to feel like they will never be loved again when they leave. This is also called *negging* in the pickup artist community. There is a reason that these men who are all suspiciously not in fulfilling relationships peddle this to a certain type of single man. It relies on the woman on the other side having a damaged or naive view of relationships that they could potentially trap and erode further. It will not work on the average person because it is abusive in its underlying theory.

Isolation

Soon you might find yourself hanging out with your old friends and family as you proceed with the relationship. They might even start talking even worse about your old circle. The point is that they want you to depend on them and have as much control over your social circle as possible.

People that have known you for years can see if you are changing for the worst. They will see it in your body language and the things you describe. Rarely is there no sign that someone will go on to do bad things. There is always a story about how the person was abusive to an animal, spoke to them demeaningly, or had a violent streak. A smitten person may miss specific phrases, veiled insults, or oddly controlling behavior. Still, their mother, best friend, or anyone else may spot the changes and put it together because they have no bias toward the abuser or have the abuser been able to charm them. It is in the best interest of a narcissistic partner to keep their possession as far away from other influences as possible.

A person will be further isolated through financial abuse. They may be encouraged to stop working and take care of the house or have a large gift held over their head. They will come to depend on their income because they have no choice in the matter, and if they leave, they feel like they have nothing. With complete social isolation, a person might be blind to a network of people willing to help.

How Do I Deal With a Narcissist?

Dealing with a narcissist who is actively harming you may be one of the hardest things you can overcome. It is no longer about stigma; a person actively abusing and taking advantage of people needs to be dealt with, and their personality will be a challenge. There will never be accountability, you cannot appeal to their better angels, and there is nothing you can do to fix them. People with narcissistic tendencies often need intense therapy by a professional. Even then, if they were never taught empathy as a child, they will never develop as adults. Once a person begins to like having power over someone else, it's over. If you recognize you are in the presence of a narcissistic abuser, congratulations, you have broken the spell they have placed on you. If you can leave, for your sanity, do so. However, if you are stuck with this person, you can try a few tactics.

Document Document Document

While it may feel pointless to document every interaction, you have to protect yourself legally and professionally. Take notes on every incident, no matter how small, date it, and include how you felt and any tangible consequences. Discreetly have any witnesses and back this file up. You have to weave a story as well since, as we will discuss later, facts are boring. In a work setting, this has to be done carefully. A pattern of behavior must be visible to shatter the illusion that this charismatic person is actually a malignant force in everyone's lives. The consequences should be framed in how the work has suffered, not how much of a victim you are; when you make yourself a victim, the powers that be often get annoyed. They don't want to hear the drama and may see you as petulant and jealous. This behavior must hurt their bottom line.

Be Careful Who You Trust

Successful people with narcissistic tendencies did not get to where they were because they were a jerk to everyone. They learned to charm the people they saw as necessary. They only have so much emotional energy to manipulate and want a return on their investment. Direct supervisors, consequential people at work, investors, and potential sexual conquests will never see the narcissists' fangs until they have used that person up. These people have no reason to believe that a person they consider a friend has been lying to them all this time. Humans tend to respond and examine good qualities over bad ones, especially when trust has come into the mix.

It may be lonely, but you may not be able to go to mutual friends or coworkers; you risk them being turned against you. Building a case takes secrecy; any ounce that something is off will dispatch alarm bells. They will try and get a head, sew discontent and distrust, and because this person likely has more influence, they might get away with it. If you are going to shoot the king, you better not miss.

Play Dead

Part of deriving fun from a person's pain is the act of watching them struggle. Some people like watching someone squirm under their shoes as they threaten you or just make you uncomfortable. They are a cat playing with a bird they caught in the backyard. It gets more thrills when it screams, flaps its wings, and tries to peck away. You cannot give in to your baser instincts to yell, insult, or even quip (unless you know you are really good at that). Don't give them anything. If they insult or threaten you just act disinterested, keep tapping at your keyboard, water a plant and dismiss them with a simple "is that all" or "okay." Over time they might get bored and they will move on.

Recognizing a Bad Apology

Narcissists will say anything to manipulate you into forgiving them. They might insist that they will change and do better, but the reality is, unless a person tangibly changes then those are hollow words. Actions always speak louder. Someone can apologize and continue doing what they were before, because change does not benefit them, plus it's hard work. Why do any of that when you can just keep saying things like:

- *You are the love of my life; I would do anything to keep you.*

- *You have to forgive me.*

- *I promise I'll do better!*

- *I can change, you just have to give me a chance!*

There is also the tact of apologizing, but minimizing the damage done. Someone apologizing to you should never make you feel guilty. It is a ploy to end the awkward conversation as fast as possible while also slowly robbing you of the ability to stand up for yourself. Phrases that make you feel crazy are:

- *Why are you so dramatic, it's not a big deal!*

- *I'm sorry if I offended you.*

- *It was just a joke!*

Phrases like these take no accountability. It shifts blame to the wronged party for feeling a certain type of way about an action. Even in an apology, a narcissist may be incapable of admitting wrongdoing.

What Have We Learned?

- Allowing the wrong person to be privy to your weaknesses gives them the book on how to manipulate you.

- You do not always need to be brought down to be manipulated, playing to someone's ego will also get them dancing in the palm of your hand.

- Recognize signs such as love-bombing, isolation, doubt, and if a loved one tells you something is off, believe them.

- Abusers will guilt, manipulate, and lie to keep themselves in your life. They dangle their ideal selves in front of you hoping you will take the bait. It is an illusion.

- Dealing with a narcissist is delicate work. You have to keep notes, keep to yourself, and make yourself a less entertaining target if you are stuck with them.

- Leave a narcissist first chance you get.

EMOTIONAL MANIPULATION
SEE IT, FLIP IT, OR USE IT TO GET WHAT YOU WANT

"When we allow another to alter out
thinking, it can take a long time to return to
our previous reality. That's the awesome
power of manipulation"

– RYAN JAMES

People can be swayed by a number of things to make
them more agreeable. Knowing when to play to a
person's ego or displaying you are not to be messed
with are vital to getting results and maybe even
keeping you out of trouble.

Sometimes to get a person's guard down, you have to
hide certain things, mirror, and keep a poker face. This
tends to work better in situations when you know you
don't have leverage. Likewise, when you are the one
with the power, it is better to affirm that rather than
letting people take even an inch.

Using Someone Else's Ego to Get the Ideal Result

When people know they have power, they are either incredibly secure in that fact or, if they are in a more precarious position, are awfully defensive. Challenging that power is not the way to get what you want when you are at a disadvantage. While you may disagree, be more suited to the work or display your dismay at the situation, there are better ways to get your point across though it might be at the sacrifice of your own ego. That's the game you have to play sometimes and you have to ask yourself: *do you want to be right or do you want to get what you want?*

Disguise Your Benefit as Their Benefit — The Power of Reframing

People respond better to your needs when it benefits them as well. If you go in making demands, it's easy to be shut down, but if you reframe what you want as a win-win, you are more likely to get your way. This is easy if you have something of equal value to offer. If you need a day off, offer to swap shifts with someone instead of putting it on the board directly. If there is a chore you hate, see if your roommate also has a chore they hate and swap; you get the idea.

You can take it a step further and disguise how much you benefit. For example, say you want a four-day work week, you will still work the same hours, but you will get a precious day off in return. Marching into your boss' office and laying it out because you prefer the schedule will not work because it can be seen as special treatment, and you have not outlined what the boss gets. Instead, frame it as an efficiency improvement:

- *I think working four ten-hour days is better because I can get more done in ten hours of work than breaking up the work to fit an eight-hour day.*

To increase the odds of the request being granted try the *foot in the door technique.* This is using a small request to lead up to asking for something much larger. Ask for a test period to see if your idea will work and if you can "handle it" (even though you already know you can). Like putting the product in your manager's hands it is difficult to argue with good results.

Prime the Pump for a Yes

Getting someone to agree to a big change can be a daunting task. Their heads might be filled with doubt and negativity initially about taking any sort of financial risk. You can prop up the idea of a positive response by using the *three yes technique*. It is seen in sales and hostage negotiations alike. The idea is to get a person to comply by asking easier questions or making simple requests. In the hostage negotiation just saying:

"Let everyone go and turn yourself in"

Is a terrible way to negotiate and without any other strategy, your agency will be in the news for a week and will have a lot of paperwork and lawsuits to settle. Instead, they approach the hostage taker by asking for easy things first.

"Put me on the phone with the woman"

"Stand by the door"

"Give me a sign everyone is okay"

This compels the hostage taker to start to agree with the negotiator. Thanks to the scale of this decision it takes a lot of compliance (upwards of twenty requests) to get to the point of getting them to free their leverage. Other methods include letting the hostage taker make choices. Things like what food they would like and people they can call.

The same can be applied to a sale but three questions with a positive are normally enough.

First, you get the story from your customer to help tailor your question. Figure out their issue and what will best work for their problem and your sale, and work backward from there. Let's say you are selling a landscaping service.

"Don't you think keeping a well-manicured lawn is exhausting?"

"Wouldn't it be easier to hire a service that will make your lawn the envy of the neighborhood?"

"Would you like to try a trial service at a discounted price?"

Part of this strategy involves reframing. Spending money is a big ask especially if you are selling in person. A person can't really pull out their phone and look at reviews, not to mention people are naturally a bit wary of strange salespeople. A potential customer will potentially see an associate there to just push their product and make their commission. People casually shopping normally do not go "I hope a salesperson corners me." You put the idea of the benefit and get the person to agree with you before the official pitch.

The same can be done with convincing a partner of a big purchase. If you want to buy a house and the other wants to rent, emphasize the benefits and prompt them to agree.

"Wouldn't the extra space and yard be nice?"

"Property is a great investment; don't you think that it could be a great way to make our money grow?"

"Do you want to start looking into buying a house?"

Don't invalidate their worries because they might not feel heard just emphasize how the benefits outweigh their reservations. You can take it a step further and put the product in their hands.

"Let's go to some open houses just to see what's out there and dream a little"

"Wanna go to the dealership and test drive a few cars?"

Remember, we are transactional creatures, and getting someone to agree to something takes having something to offer, even if the other person was not aware of it.

Making People Think Your Idea Was Their Idea

This is good when you need something done but you are not the person to make that decision. You may be lower on the totem pole or they may be in a position of power. Either way, it might be hard to convince them of something. One way to do this is to frame your idea as a question. You will look like you are deferring to their opinion when in fact you are planting an idea in their head. If they reject it you never challenged their authority but if they see reason they can get the credit and you can make your life easier.

This can also work in the work environment. Say a plan made by a higher-up is flawed, maybe the assignments aren't balanced, maybe a technique is not efficient or maybe another client should have more priority. Instead of directly challenging their points, try reframing your concerns as you try to clear up your own confusion with a question.

- *How should we prioritize this in relation to our other clients?*

- *Why are we using this technique/tool, shouldn't we use this one because of...*

- *Don't you think we should bring this person on? They have experience in this and it would benefit the project.*

Plus if the plan works the boss might remember how observant you were in the question. If they don't listen and their plan fails, then they might be keener to listen to your idea plus you were just doing what the boss said. Being visible like this will get you ahead in life without having to fight too much for your place in the hierarchy.

Why People Get Ahead

If you decided to pursue this book you have probably been in a position where you felt like you were passed over. It happens more to a certain type of person, especially in the workforce. There is a game to be played here and you might not like certain aspects of it, but the people that engage with this game are the ones to get ahead and put their friends ahead.

You Are Probably Approaching Your Work All Wrong

Let's create a fictional work environment that mirrors most corporate environments in the United States. This company has technical applications valued and necessary in the production goals; it can be coding, editing, or anything that has a tangible skill being used to meet company goals. This company is medium in size, with defined departments (technical, customer-facing, sales, etc.), workers, managers, an HR department, and a very defined company culture. Everyone works in the same building in a major city.

You, the reader, are in a technical position working in a small team answering to a manager. You take pride in your work and have done so since day one. You were eager to show everyone that you could do the job quickly and correctly. To meet the manager's now high expectations of you, you often need to skip happy hours and meetings you deem unnecessary, show up to the meetings you are required to attend right on time, and book it out of there at the earliest time. You show up to work a bit more casual than most, with a t-shirt and jeans, but you are not customer-facing, and no one has ever called you out. You don't have any friends in the company, but that's okay! You are there to get a job done, and these people honestly seem kind of annoying. You are content spending your precious free time decompressing on your own. When your annual review comes around, you get glowing remarks and are one of the top performers. You are very proud, and you feel validated in your approach.

Suddenly your manager announces that he is retiring. You realize that this could be a step up, there is more pay, more PTO[1], and you get a lot more sway in

---

[1] PTO: Acronym for Paid Time Off.

decisions. This department is relatively new, and everyone has been around for roughly the same time. You realize that you are a shoo-in for the manager position because they want to keep the hire internal, and you know the job and the department inside and out. You apply and interview with the higher-ups. The interview goes as well as expected; you keep it professional, demonstrate your technical knowledge and assure them that you can handle a small team working under you. A week later, they announce the decision, and you find out the most unlikely candidate usurped you... let's call him Chet.

Chet started working about a month after you. He had decent technical skills, but he was not as efficient, nor did he have your expertise. Still, from what you could tell, he was pretty well-liked. He greeted everyone the second they walked into the room, made it to what seemed like every happy hour, and constantly made small talk with everyone. He had an uncanny ability to remember details about people's personal lives, and even you have to admit...you actually found the guy pleasant to be around, albeit in small doses. His excellent memory and weird ability to make consistent eye contact bothered you, but he was popular. Not to mention despite not being an efficient worker, he always had time to wear an ironed button-up, slacks, and even a tie. His hair looked like butter on toast, and his perfect beard framed his even more perfect smile beautifully (or so the ladies at work said). He was the life of the party at the work retreat that you skipped because frolicking in the woods with your coworkers frankly didn't appeal to you.

Still, despite all his good points, him being your boss was an outrage. He never worked at the pace you did, never reached a benchmark ahead of schedule, the boss never asked him to do extra work, and never did supplemental training that would have made him better in his technical role. You are asking yourself how you let yourself lose to Chet, of all people, a mediocre performer through it all. That can't be right, can it?

How to Avoid Being the Job Pack Mule Instead of the Show Pony

So you the reader are now stuck answering to Chet for the foreseeable future, after stewing on it for a bit you realized that in your pursuit to be the best in your role, you have inadvertently sabotaged yourself in several ways. Chet on the other hand played the game like a pro because he had a goal in mind and did not feel the need to prove himself to anyone other than the higher-ups.

You Showed Off Your Full Potential From Day One

This is a mistake a lot of young, eager, and talented employees make. They want to save the day immediately, so the second they get good at their job, they take their talents as far as possible. They tell their boss, "look at how much I got done in a time crunch," "I applied this skill you had no idea I had to fill this gap you didn't even know was there." Revealing your speed or all your abilities right off the bat is a mistake. The higher-ups will get used to that level of work and will become resentful when you can't sustain it. After all, they might not have even asked for that level, but you had to show it off. You can only be in that gear for so long, and the enthusiasm for that new job sustains it. But soon, life gets in the way, and you burn out. If the job comes to rely on that, you are in trouble, and it is your fault because you volunteered that information.

Do not be a hero when you are new, especially if you are starting at an entry-level position. You are the lowest person on the totem pole, and expectations are not that high. This might be a blow to your pride, but you can use this to your advantage. Meet and maybe slightly exceed expectations within your stated responsibilities. Embrace the freemium version of you! During this time, decide what you want your future to be. Do you want to be a technical manager, or do you want to go even higher? There may come a time when you become so efficient at your job that you might have some free time.

Do not volunteer for any work that does not benefit you in this spare time.

People may see that you are getting good at your work and may start asking you to help them with their projects. For example, a separate department needed a bit of help catching up with some technical write-ups. They asked both you and Chet to help. Chet politely declined to state that he had too much on his plate at the moment but recommended you because you had mentioned you used to do similar writing at a previous job. You say yes since you were new and wanted to be seen as a team player, plus you were stuck because you showed your hand too quickly. Suddenly you were asked to help out constantly. It was low-level work that you were now obligated to do, that is not shown off at meetings and only serves to help another department that you have no interest in joining in fulfilling their quota. It is outside your scope, and you have to work a little bit later to keep up with not only your responsibilities but also the emergencies of other people.

On the other hand, Chet attended management seminars, hung around before and after meetings to talk to people, went to the gym, and got a full night's sleep because he was not taking work home with him.

Chet did not mention that he used to do freelance work as a technical writer. After his assigned work was done, he often had a couple of hours to spare and worked on honing his ability to write pitch decks and take online classes with certificates that he could put on his resume. Chet kept his potential under his hat, investing in his future while you invested in the present, which killed any hope of getting promoted.

Never Make Yourself Indispensable

If you have been a talent in your job, but it has never led to promotion, this is probably why. Why would the company take someone so dependable in one job sector and put them elsewhere where they are not proven? Why would they train someone else to fill in that new gap when you are right there? You have to be strategic in managing others' expectations of you. If there is a whole department emergency and a strategic place to be the hero, show your hand. Chalk it up to rising to the occasion and realizing potential you were unaware of (it's not like they can prove otherwise). If it is another department's problem and you don't stand to gain anything (it is vital to ensure no opportunities here), don't bother, even if it means they are drowning. It's not your fault, nor is it your responsibility. It would be a kind thing, but it can pave the way to getting pigeon hold. You want to be good enough that people respect you but not so good that you are relied upon. Since Chet got his work done, he was also able to play the game that many people hate in the corporate world.

Make Sure People Love You

Here is the cheat code to getting what you want in life. It sounds obvious, but life is easier when people like you. People will be more willing to help you, give you grace when you mess up, and will take risks for you. Unless you were born to inherit a company, you have to play the game of knowing who specifically to give your energy to. Your main focus should be your immediate circle and higher-ups. Make sure you get close to your team and anyone that might have any sway in your future. It does not have to be too in-depth and there are a few easy ways to do that quickly.

1. Take an interest in their jobs and ask them questions about them. People love to be deferred to for their expertise. So long as you are not a pest about it, you can stroke their ego a bit and get some good mentorship. A word of caution though, use this sparingly and avoid chatter boxes even if they are experts: you don't want to get stuck all day.

2. Show up to meetings early and sit facing the door. You can greet people easily and it's a

great way to establish rapport. Also, it never feels good to be ignored when entering a room. It can be unintentional but it can be isolating. You can be the social butterfly that makes an effort to be nice. Plus you won't get stuck in a pointless conversation because the meeting will interrupt it.

3. While you want to make yourself visible by asking questions at meetings, do not be a gunner or the person to ask deliberately difficult questions just to sound smart. If there is a critical issue, then by all means (and when in doubt, remember to frame that as a question), but no one likes the gunner. You can always ask the person in private. They will appreciate your discretion and you won't be that guy to make meetings longer.

4. Listen to people vent but NEVER engage in gossip. You don't know who will be friends one day then enemies the next then make up the next day. If you are caught trash-talking then your head can be on the chopping block. People like a sympathetic ear plus it's a great way to gather information. If someone is upset if you ask some tactful follow-up questions they won't stop talking.

5. Go to the happy hours when you know people you want to get close to are attending. I know these can be a drag but it can get important people to trust you on a deeper level which can give you an edge in the workplace. Once they start telling you about their personal lives you have an in.

None of these things involve becoming best friends, pulling all-nighters, or sucking up in front of all your colleagues. They are, on the surface, just incredibly baseline and strategic socializing. You don't have to care about Patty in HR's neuralgia or Tom in IT's kids but letting them talk about it in controlled settings will endear them to you.

Maybe one day Patty can put a good word in for you for a promotion or Tom will be willing to stay late fixing your computer problems so you can meet your deadline. Since people like you and see a bit of themselves in people they like, they will attribute that mistake to human error (the way they see their shortcomings) instead of incompetence, laziness, or stupidity. Plus once you have someone's trust, it is difficult to break so long as you are not consistently awful.

How to Use Psychology to See Where You Stand

Workplace relationships can be very shallow. While there are close knit groups, for the most part you are going to be dealing with people that are putting on the same pleasantries that you are in hopes of making the work as easy as possible. As such, it is easier to lie to you. This makes seeing how you are perceived, and your future in the company a little blurry. Remember there are ways you can cut through the words and see what people are thinking.

- Do they regard you with respect to the future? If you are not long for the team or are just not respected, people are less regarded to talk about you regarding future plans. They will not ask you about your goals or their vision of you in a higher position.

- Are there private meetings or group chats? Socially this is to be expected. It may hurt but it only says how coworkers see you in a social setting. However if there are meetings or chats that involve your work and you are not a part of it, that is a problem. It sets you up for failure if there is a communication breakdown. Also if there are changes in expectations that you are

116

not aware of because it is not in writing, you can end up looking bad.

- Do people regularly go over your head? This is not only annoying, but it shows a complete disregard for your opinion. If someone is constantly trying to confirm your decisions with management "to make sure" that might be something to look into.

- Are you the butt of the joke at meetings? There is a place for ribbing every now and then, but in a formal setting in front of everyone is not it. Being singled out constantly only serves to demean you for the purpose of elevating someone's ego.

There are also a couple of ways to see if you are earning the respect of others that do not rely on blind praise.

- Are people mirroring you? People tend to mirror those they like and who they respect if they are in a room with a lot of people.

- If you are at a rectangular table see how people sit in relation to you if you are leading the meeting. Leaders tend to sit at the head of the table. The people who feel like they are second in command sit next to the leader. The worker bees sit in the middle. The one that is more apt to challenge you tends to sit directly in front of you to get face time. If the same person is sitting across from you every time and chooses that seat they might be gunning for you. It might not be antagonistic and you might even have another perspective to gain insight.

- Do people talk to you about their private lives? This indicates that they trust you beyond the level of a coworker. It might not be at the level of "friend" but that level of casualness is a good sign, especially if that person is above you.

What Have We Learned

- Getting what you want is more important than showing people you are in control or have influence.

- Try not to challenge those above you, instead frame your suggestions as questions and let the person come to the obvious solution.

- Get people agreeing with you right off the bat with easy and obvious questions. This makes them more open to more involved ideas and requests.

- Manage people's expectations of you early on. Don't be the hero in a new environment, allow yourself room to appear as if you are growing.

- Don't just covet the promotion, act and dress in a way that makes people be able to see you in that role.

A CON-NOISSEUR MAN

"The secret of being a top-notch con man is
being able to know what the mark wants,
and how to make him think he's getting it."

– KEN KESEY

Cons come in all shapes and sizes and are aimed at the
most vulnerable. There are several strategies to
maximize their victim base.

- Play it as a numbers game so that you
  eventually get someone who is fooled.

- Going out and seeking random people that fit
  a certain profile.

- Reframing their scam as something that will
  benefit someone with a specific problem or
  goal.

A Nigerian Prince Casts a Wide Net

The simplest scams involve just trying your pitch on everyone and seeing who falls for it. When the internet became popular so did the occurrence of scams. The classic is the old Nigerian Prince email. A foreign prince wants to give you money...lucky you right? Well, that "prince" is probably in a computer mill surrounded by a hundred other "princes."

It's funny now but people who were not familiar with the internet were not aware that people could just boldly lie to them. Another party having your personal email was infeasible so obviously, this must be important.

The Nigerian prince is basically a meme at this point but its variants still exist. While the prince uses FOMO more scams use scare tactics to target the elderly. It seems like the second someone starts collecting social security checks their chances of being scammed increase. Calls involving delinquent bills, the IRS, and incorrect filings are all common. They scare a person and then tell their victim that everything will be okay so long as you give them all their banking information.

Old people are often unaware that a company would never ask you for your info over the phone and if you are dealing with late payments, they would mail you about it. The elderly are vulnerable to their lack of tech savviness and fixed income.

Luckily, this con is pretty obvious, ignore the email or robocall and go about your day. Be sure to educate the less tech-savvy people in your life to not trust someone so freely just because they call or email with an urgent message.

Staying Vigilant to Protect Yourself — Conmen on the Street

A lot of crimes require very little thought or planning. Sometimes someone just sees something they want and knows they can take it from you very easily. We already discussed how looking like a tourist can make you a prime suspect for scams. There are other signals you can be flashing tourists or not that can make you a target. Unfortunately, some of these you can't help but know about them can potentially keep you safe.

Don't Look Lost or Distracted

The classic sign that a person is confused and vulnerable. It is very easy to spot someone who has no idea where they are. They will constantly be looking up skyscrapers, buried in their phone, or turn around once they realize they have gone the wrong way. They will most likely also be grimacing and look worried. If you are distracted you will not notice someone taking the wallet out of your jacket, rifling through your purse, or someone getting too close and yanking the phone right out of your hand. By the time you get your bearings and realize what has happened, they are gone.

Looking lost also means you might not be aware of common scams employed that the locals are wise to. Locals will know to avoid people aggressively selling bracelets, but a tourist will be caught off guard when someone puts a bracelet on their wrist and demands payment. Most will give in. There is also the New York City mixtape scam which works the same way; someone will hand you a mixtape and the second it is in your hand they will demand money for it and tourists are so scared they comply.

More often than not if you look out of place and it can be assumed that you have something valuable, you will be hit with overwhelming force and have a weapon in your face. If you are lost outside do not also get lost in your phone, keep it tucked away and check for directions in a more public space or duck into a store.

Try and Carry Yourself with Confidence

Posture can give criminals a peek inside your mindset and physical health to let them know if you are an easy mark. A slouched posture or a strange gait (the way you walk) can signal that you might not be at your physical best. In short, they can see you are physically weaker, which first might distract you but second make it so you can't give chase. It can also signal a lack of confidence which can play into whether a person will fight hard or tell anyone what occurred. Looking down, frazzled or unsure, and trying to look invisible will do the opposite of what you want. Instead, walk as if you belong there, confident and, most importantly, relaxed. Looking too rigid will also make you stick out. The key is not to set yourself apart from the crowd, what makes a crime of opportunity is a unique target. There are no guarantees but this can help you keep a low profile and in turn keep you safe.

Never Allow Someone to Enter Your Bubble

Once you let someone into your personal space, you have lost the first game. A lot of scams and crimes cannot occur if you just keep walking. However, once they get that level of engagement, getting out of trouble can be more difficult, and depending on the person's intentions, you can be in a lot of danger. This is not limited to touch; eye contact is the first level of contact that a person permits and it swings open the gates for more.

This is a common tactic for aggressive panhandlers; they will go in a public space, they will be loud, and act erratically all to get someone's attention. Once they have it they will pester, beg, shame, pressure, and swear to get you to give them money so they can leave you alone. If you feel vulnerable it is okay to just look straight ahead (if you are in an enclosed space your phone can give you an out) and not engage. You do not owe any one time or attention and no amount of pestering will change that. If it goes wrong, all it does is tell people you are easily disarmed, and they can invade your space even more.

If a stranger gets you engaged their next step may be to change your plans also known as taking you to another location. If you tell a panhandler that you don't carry cash and they tell you they know where an ATM is, turn around and get away. Once you deviate and go with a stranger even if they look harmless any number of things can await you like an accomplice with a weapon or an isolated area that makes harming you a much more private affair.

The *law of reciprocity* can make a person feel like they have no choice but to let someone invade their space. This is our second psychological human weakness: when someone gives us something, no matter how minor, we feel obligated to provide them with something in return. Whether it's money, time, or a favor, once that exchange is made we tend to be more malleable to another person's desires and people are aware of this. Some people may take this to an extreme and hold the tiniest thing over your head then shame you into giving them more than the value of their offer.

Practice Defusing These Interactions

You will run into someone who will want something from you at some point. If you live in a city it is most likely a daily occurrence. Whether it's money, time or attention they will pull a lot of tricks to squeeze something out of you. There are some things you should avoid

- Reacting with hostility: You don't want to agitate a person who might already be desperate (desperation can be very dangerous if you don't know how to deal with it) and if there is a crowd you do not want them to potentially turn on you if they misread the interaction. Also, some of these people asking for help might genuinely be in dire situations. It costs nothing to be kind—always be cautious.

- Giving too many details or excuses: You don't want to give a complete stranger any information about who you are, where you are going, and if you are alone. If you make up an excuse they will try to skirt around the excuse to pressure you into further interaction ("oh you don't drink, how about coffee"). Furthermore, you want to limit your time with them, time is money and to them, more interaction means more time used up means they might be more invested in this interaction.

- Placating or compromising: There is no middle ground either they get your money/attention or they don't. Likewise, this person is a stranger and you have nothing to gain from them.

- Don't fall for their guilt trip or sob story: Even if they spent time with you, built rapport, or made contact you still owe this person nothing. They will accuse you of being greedy, wasting their time, or being heartless. Using shame is incredibly effective when friendliness is out the window.

There are a few skills and phrases you should keep in your back pocket if you are approached by an over-eager salesman, con artist, or all-around creep.

- It's not enough to be alert, you have to look alert: Put the phone away, keep the big headphones off and walk like you know where you are going even if you are completely lost. If you feel yourself tense up, ask yourself how you would walk on the sidewalk in front of your home. Tell everyone you belong there.

- If you are trapped on a subway with a person making a scene, do not engage, do not look up, once you do that you have set yourself apart from the rest.

- If someone offers anything you do not want or ask for, like a drink, a note, or a "gift," a simple "no thank you" will suffice. No is a complete sentence and it shuts down the conversation most times. It is most effective when it is quick and authoritative. Your body language can help; putting your hands out further cements that you are actively keeping them at a distance. If someone pesters you further that's when you walk away either to people you may know or a person in authority like a bartender or security guard.

- Other phrases that are gentle but unambiguous are:

  - *Sorry I don't carry cash*

  - *It's not personal but I would like to be left alone*

  - *I can't help you*

  - *I'm not interested in what you are selling*

- Keep walking, they can't hook you in if you are always in motion.

All these tips can help protect you from quick crimes and scams perpetrated by strangers who saw an opportunity. In contrast, these can help you, it's no secret that stranger danger is the least of your worries. Unfortunately, as children, we were only taught to look for shady men in trench coats and robbers wearing masks. People that we know and trust can victimize us twice, once from the crime itself, and the other by betraying the trust we let them foster.

Selling a Fantasy, not a Product

One of the most effective sales tactics does not involve selling the product at all, it's about selling a story. Investors, CEOs, and gurus of every ilk have mastered the art of tricking a person into opening their wallet based on how they feel about a fantasy that was just presented to them. It is a very effective way to pull the wool over the public's eyes when the product either isn't going right or is an outright scam. There are a few framing devices for these dream weavers:

- The CEOs themselves are these inspirational, superhuman figures who will change the world. A person is more willing to climb aboard because they are being seduced by a cult of personality they admire.

- The product or service will do something revolutionary and be a net positive for humanity (think charities or providing VC funding for a start-up).

- The product or service will not only perform unrealistic miracles but will also fill a hole in a person's life.

More than one of these can be employed at a time by the same company but the result is the same. The product gets funded, pre-ordered and stocks are bought. If the product works, great but if not the rug will get pulled and the investors and customers will be left with nothing.

One of the most insidious things that CEOs promise is that their MLM[2] or class will change a person overnight. They use the grifter's triad of fear, opportunity, and shame to bamboozle desperate people into getting suckered into their scheme.

Little does the poor sap know that they most likely will never see any return on their investment. If anything they will lose out on time, money, and when the dust settles, their self-esteem.

---

[2] MLM: Acronym for Multi-Level Marketing

I Have a Proposition That Will Change Your Life

Humans are simple creatures and they stake their self-esteem on things that bring them status. Wealth, influence, and a strong social circle, if someone lacks any of these it is difficult for them to feel like they have achieved self-actualization. They may feel suffocated by their role as stay-at-home moms, insecure in their role in the house, and long to bring in income. They can be someone who feels emasculated because he can't get a date or because he has not been able to afford all the material possessions they think will make them a desirable person.

Enter the guru, the all-perfect, all-knowing teacher that will give you everything you have ever wanted and more. They have ads promoting a class, business opportunity, or consulting service. These can be anything, pick-up artist classes, selling leggings, diets, and all manner of get-quick-rich schemes. The product is secondary though, what they are actually selling is hope bottled in a five-part class.

You see the guru's social media and you start comparing their life to yours and you start to feel pretty inadequate. They have a picture-perfect family, a sterile-looking house, cars, money and they look happy. There is also often the promise of community.

A class filled with like-minded people all helping each other gain the same thing. If it's a book or a PDF plan, this is enough for people to get out their credit cards. They get that dopamine hit when they purchase the product because they feel like their life is about to change for the better. The practice is even more effective when the guru is active in the community.

A lot of these seminars and classes are flashy and leave a crowd euphoric. The guru comes out to loud upbeat music, there are spotlights, the occasional smoke machine, and a slide show of the guru's accomplishments. They whip up the crowd and then explain how once upon a time they were a loser too; until they discovered the secret to fill that hole in their soul that everyone in the crowd seems to share. Male gurus sometimes take the role of a paternal figure for the men in their community. They dispel advice in a very fatherly way knowing that some of the men have felt emasculated by life. A mark will be sold on the dream so quickly that they don't consider the consequences of their investment.

Wooed by the promise of being a mom who is also a girl boss earning enough money to go on vacations, the stay-at-home might start purchasing MLM products to sell. They were just fooled into joining a pyramid scheme where they are on the bottom and will most likely never make any money. Their only hope is to recruit friends and family; dooming them to the same fate. They will never be able to sell the product because it is almost always inevitably low quality. Plus if a specific MLM has infiltrated a certain town, they are also working against over saturation of both product and participants. Only when they have run out of money and realize they have a garage full of products they will never be able to sell do they realize they have made a terrible mistake.

This pattern repeats itself over and over and is not limited to having to do labor and sell. Any legitimate financial advisor will tell you that investing is a long-term game. You put your money in index funds and don't look at it for a few years. The problem—it's boring and takes forever, you want money now! Nowadays it seems like everyone has a hot new stock tip or a new crypto coin that will revolutionize capitalism as we know it. It requires next to no effort to take your hard-earned money and entrust it to these "investors." The excitement of easy money (this is gambling) and the hit of dopamine you get by making the investment can lead to a very impulsive and expensive decision. If someone is giving out tips to the masses, it's only to inflate the price for those who bought the stock cheaply. Those on the ground floor will sell high, tanking the price of a stock they artificially inflated. Since the only real value of the stock or coin came from hype and nothing tangible, there is often no hope of recovering your loss. All people can do is post their loss on investor forums, commiserate with each other, and hope the next tip will make them rich.

Lessons From Monsters #5:
When Fake it 'Till You Make it Goes Wrong, Elizabeth Holmes

The story of Elizabeth Holmes and Theranos is a cautionary one. Investors spent billions on a product that never existed and is proof of how the phrase *fake it till you make it* can only take you so far if you cannot produce results before people get suspicious.

Elizabeth Holmes had a dream, part of it was revolutionizing the laboratory testing industry, but it was mostly to be someone important. She had an idea; Elizabeth was set on inventing a device that could run hundreds of medical tests on a single drop of blood. She took these aspirations and founded Theranos. Elizabeth hired engineers and techs to make her dream a reality.

She just needed the funding since developing biotechnology is monstrously expensive. She tried running the idea by a few actual biologists, but they all shot her down because the technology could never work. In need of a runway, Elizabeth concocted a plan to get people to believe in her vision without proof by selling them on helping her change the world.

Instead of experts in the biotech field, Elizabeth recruited influential men in government and business for her board. Her board included Henry Kissenger, James Mattis, and Howard Shultz, all of whom were career politicians. These weren't scientists who could check the merits of her work; they were yes-men with deep pockets that Elizabeth could charm. Elizabeth would tell them a story about how the outdated, bloated, scary, and unaffordable Big Lab Corporations could be made obsolete.

Elizabeth was known for her striking eye contact; people alleged that she barely blinked, and it felt like she was staring into your soul. Her femininity was a liability, so she modeled herself after Steve Jobs. She sported black turtlenecks and pants every day. Jobs famously did the same, stating that it gave him one less thing to worry about in the morning. She also started to deepen her voice whenever she spoke in public. No one at the time really questioned the tactics, but it was actually brilliant.

While her technology was new, she made herself seem familiar in the CEO space to inspire more trust. She disarmed these investors with a sweet story, the chance to be an early investor in a revolutionary company, and they gave her billions. The only problem, her staff could not get the technology to work.

Getting the newly dubbed *Edison Machine* to work in the lab was a nightmare. The machine not only could not run tests reliably, but it was a safety hazard as the technicians risked getting stuck with bloody needles, and it caught fire at one point. All those scientists were right; the idea behind the technology was infeasible. This did not deter Holmes, who needed to impress to get more funding. She had technicians dilute blood samples (an obscene breach of lab protocol) and cherry-pick data.

As the company moved forward, experienced techs quit when they saw the writing on the wall. They were replaced with recent college graduates who were not only under Holmes' spell but were also too young to know how a proper laboratory is supposed to function.

As marketing worked on promising the sun and the moon to anyone who would invest in *The Edison* and the lab were literally putting out fires, Elizabeth continued to gain influence. She was famous as a woman in STEM who started a billion-dollar company. She regularly rubbed elbows with the most prominent players in the tech world. Then Vice President Joe Biden even interviewed her!

She kept control of the company by selling the staff on her cult of personality and how much good the company would do. She insisted every worker was helping her change the world. There were cult-like all-hands meetings, a typically absurd silicon valley office/lab space to work in, and parties to keep the workers happy. However, there was a dark side to the office. Everyone knew they were getting keystrokes; no communication was private. The marketing and lab departments were kept separate and not allowed to interact. Thanks to this isolation level, the marketing team had no idea how dire the lab situation was.

When tours were given, the lab was on its best behavior. This is pretty typical when investors tour the places their cash is in, but in the case of Theranos, there was a sinister undercut. Holmes would give the tour and let one of the investors get a drop of their blood tested on *The Edison*. In reality, a tech would grab the sample out of the machine, test the blood with a standard protocol and load up the results, all while the tour was having lunch. It was all a magic trick, and no one was the wiser. That is until Holmes decided to fly too close to the sun.

The decision to put a completely untested machine in Walgreens started the destruction of Theranos. Walgreens fell for the ruse hook, line, and sinker, and they wanted to get in on the action. They put these machines in their stores and had real people use them for diagnostic testing. Lab protocols were flagrantly ignored to get any results back to the patients. The tests were so unreliable that patients did not only test negative and were never informed that they were sick, but some were even told they had cancer. The numbers were so ludicrous that many patients were sent to the emergency room for fear of dying.

The disastrous Walgreens deal and some internal whistle-blowers finally tore Theranos down. Elizabeth was the emperor who had no clothes and had to answer to many people from governing bodies, the patients she had harmed, and the investors she had swindled. Overnight, the billion-dollar silicon valley company was defunct, everyone was laid off, and Elizabeth had to face deposition. As she had to sheepishly admit that she had been lying for years, her cold eyes remained unblinking, possibly trying to charm someone else to no avail.

When in Doubt, Don't Sell Facts, Sell a Juicy Story

The biggest lesson you can take away from these con artists is that when the facts are not on your side, tell a story. It is the tact of aspiring CEOs, salesmen, and lawyers. Unfortunately, today's population finds facts tedious and inconvenient.

The defense changed tactics when the trial against OJ Simpson seemed like a slam dunk. Instead of arguing the damning facts that included DNA, hair, a bloody footprint, a history of domestic abuse, and the famous gloves, the defense weaved an elaborate emotional story that put the police on trial. The jury was confused by DNA since its use was relatively new, and every piece of evidence was questioned since the LAPD had a long history of racism.

It worked; the jury did not remember the complicated evidence; they remembered a story about how OJ had been the latest target of a police department with a real history of violence and racism against black people. OJ walked because of Johnny Cochran. He was charismatic, coming up with catchy phrases that the jury would easily remember, spoke like a preacher, and was able to spin a story from nothing.

It's not enough to spin a story about how great or wronged you were. You have to let the audience feel that way too. You let them dream about how much better their life could be, or how they have been wronged.

They relate with you, laugh with you, and cry with you. The emotional connection is quite intimate, but it builds trust and opens them up to trust anything you say.

What Have We Learned?

- Con-artists will use shotgun approaches to attack naive people.

- The most insidious scams target specific vulnerabilities and shame.

- Using body language and being direct will keep you from getting targeted in the open.

- Be wary of anyone that tries to sell you a story, not a product.

- When you are selling, facts alone are boring.

ROOTING OUT THE MOLE IN YOUR GROUP

"Keep your friends close, and your enemies closer."

– MICHAEL CORLEONE: THE GOD FATHER

Gathering information and even exposing moles is a lost skill. It is the year 2012, and you are enjoying the smash HBO hit Game of Thrones. There is a scene in the second season that is a master class gathering information from everyone's favorite drunken imp, Tyrion Lannister. He is in a position of power and is determined to keep it. His obstacle, though, is his sister, Cersei, who would love to see his head on a pike. Tyrion has the advantage of real power, and he knows it.

You watch as he looks at the king's inner circle and carves out weakness, opportunity, and alliances. He tests them by informing them that he plans to offer up his niece, Myrcella (also Cersei's daughter), to marry into a different noble family. He sees what each of them does with the information. Varys, the spymaster who later becomes his closest friend, does nothing of note with the information. Littlefinger, the backstabbing opportunist, does not go to the Queen; he instead goes to the family to verify the information. Finally, there was Pycelle the Grand Meister, who spills his version of the secret to Cersei to curry favor.

If you have a mole amongst you committing espionage, whether for business or someone else's gain, rooting them out secretly will protect you from any harm these people are trying to incur.

Hunting for Moles is Not Just a Spy's Game

When we think about cutting off routes of espionage we think about wartime double agents. The cold war was rife with secrets, spies, and betrayals that have filled up hundreds of books and have been the basis for movies and TV. The Soviets and the United States sent spies to each other to try and get one up on each other. Some of those spies would turn on their home country and become double agents, effectively committing treason. Moles and double agents have turned the tides of war, betrayed, lied and have gotten their colleagues killed.

Getting Your Revenge on a Mole

Has everything started to go wrong on things that are incredibly sensitive? Maybe someone is feeding information to the opposing counsel in a trial, maybe your ideas are getting stolen, maybe everyone just knows your business. This was not happening before and now you are getting suspicious.

You have started to analyze your communications for patterns and see one emerging. You have a suspect, this person you may have trusted with your confidence, or maybe they just have access to your space. You realize that information is slowly leaking after a chat or after you have been away from your space. Still, you need proof. What can you do?

Keep Feeding Them Information

It sounds counterintuitive but this tactic has been used in international espionage for decades. If you have multiple suspects you can pull the Tyrion Lannister trick and feed them slightly different information. It has to be discrete. Playing to their ego works, tell them you are trusting them with some information that is privileged. If the information in question is a document you can add a distinct tag like a codeword or a tiny symbol hidden among the pixels of an image.

Once the information comes back you will know who leaked it. Not only will this confirm who your mole is but you have kept the line of communication open. Since the mole doesn't suspect a thing, now it is your turn to mess with them.

Have Fun

You have a person who is deliberately betraying you for power or money, you can confront them and put a stop to it all, or you can ruin them. Personally, the latter sounds more fun. You can make them a liability to their handler. Keep pumping up their ego by revealing more that sounds sensitive but is actually inaccurate. Make it embarrassing.

If you are working on a project someone is trying to steal, complain about problems that don't exist, tout imaginary solutions, mess with protocols, and futz their copy of the data. They will be chasing a version of the project that does not exist, spending money and getting nowhere. No matter how well your project is doing, keep it close to the chest. Vent to your mole, run ideas by them because you trust them oh so much.

Soon you will have your mole wrapped around your finger. Before they get too suspicious that their intel is wrong you can sweeten the pie by digging through their personal life. Social media is the enemy of anyone who wants to keep a secret. Once you hear a rumor about a person, verifying it on social media is a piece of cake if they were careless. Maybe they were tagged in an embarrassing video, or maybe they had a messy affair. Things like this will discredit your mole in the eyes of everyone. Just be careful disseminating this information. Let the rumor mill run its natural course.

GASLIGHTING, REVERSE PSYCHOLOGY AND LYING TO GAIN AN ADVANTAGE

"A lie gets halfway around the world before truth puts on its boots"

– WINSTON CHURCHILL

Gaslighting and lying are very ugly words and for good reason. They historically have been used to manipulate people and keep them under the thumbs of people that are powerful. Still, by recognizing it and being able to use it, you can not only protect yourself but use it to get what you want.

Most People Are Terrible Liars

As discussed in the Nonverbal communication section of this book, people are terrible liars without even noticing. Their brains often fail to connect body and mouth, which can be pretty easy to spot. Bad acting is a blatant example of how dysphoric it can be. Two people can have the same lines. A good actor will put his whole body, tone, and subtlety to move the audience to genuine emotion. A bad actor, for example, Tommy Wiseau in *The Room,* will say the line "You are tearing me apart Lisa," but the way he performs the line does not match the scene's tone. His wife has just cheated on him, and instead of conveying sadness or disbelief with any restraint, he shouts, exaggerates his hand movements, and looks more deranged than crushed. The audience didn't feel what the director/actor/writer (all Tommy Wiseau, by the way) wanted them to handle. Lying and doing it well relies on the same principle.

Remember what we said about so-called "lying tells" there has to be context to it. You cannot just analyze a person's behavior and spot not only the lie but specific lies. Think of a lie detector test. While it is easily beaten and pseudoscience garbage it does two things well. It measures a person's vitals in real-time as questions are being asked, and it adds an extra layer of pressure since an unknowing person thinks lie detectors are foolproof.

They are not, and the results are not admissible as evidence. It is a tool that investigators can use to exhaust a suspect, break down all their hopes and defenses and get them to confess.

This is a very tricky skill to master and this book is just a drop in the bucket of information on this topic. Most honest teachers of this skill will tell you:

- This is an extremely difficult skill to learn
- It is not full proof
- It is not effective if you have not spent time with the person in question
- The tells are not proof, but they should be signs to dig deeper

Police interrogations are a treasure trove of techniques that one can look up and examine in real time. The way they arrange the room is strategic:

- They are often windowless and the police officer stands between them and the door
- The lights are turned up so it is nowhere for someone to hide
- It is cold
- It feels hostile

There's a reason that interrogation rooms and therapy offices are not designed in the same way. One relies on brute force and intimidation to get to an ugly truth, and the other depends on trust, safety, and relaxation to help with a particular problem. The strategy has two prongs:

- The suspect can never get comfortable. When someone lies they may have a tell but if they are allowed to relax they might be able to will some of those tells away.

- It sends the message that they are in trouble, and the only way out is to satisfy the detective. Essentially, they must depend on this person they see as an enemy.

There are some stories of chairs having one leg shorter than the other to also keep the suspect uncomfortable but any police department without a death wish would keep the chair bolted to the floor. A seating area that encourages movement will also encourage and even amplify the tells.

When designing your office, you can use a swivel chair to get the same effect when you want to question people (be sure they aren't the type of people that would use the chair as a weapon). Just remember your chair has to be firm on the ground so you don't accidentally broadcast your nerves.

I Spy a Lie

Most people hate and are not accustomed to lying. There are a lot of mental blocks that keep us from becoming effective at it. Knowing them allows you to spot them and avoid falling into this behavior yourself if the time comes.

You have to be familiar with that person's baseline and then compare that behavior with how they answer questions. If a person is sweating when they introduce themselves then sweating is not a very reliable tell because they might just be a sweaty person. If they maintain eye contact for the whole interview and suddenly avert when a specific question is asked, you might have something.

Other behaviors to look out for that appear suddenly include:

- Grooming (touching the hair, fixing the tie, adjusting the shirt)

- Sweating or loosening clothes- adrenaline may have suddenly raised their temperature

- Swallowing, taking a drink, or coughing once a question is asked- their mouth has gone dry, or they are buying time (doing so after an answer is probably not a concern)

- Fussing over positions on objects

- Bobbing the leg
- Wringing the hands

Word Vomit

When a person suddenly starts giving a lot of details to answer a question that does not require it, that is a bad sign. They may be trying to endear you to them by freely giving out information, but all it does is reveal a person might be defensive.

For example, say you are asked:

- *Did you cheat on me?*

An honest-sounding answer would be:

- *No! Why would you think that?*

A lie would sound like:

- *I would never cheat on you! I love you! I've been working so many hours I wouldn't have time to cheat! Who told you? Was it Becky? I knew she would turn you against me!!!*

There were a lot of words there except for the word "no." That is because of the second trap liars fall into. Word vomit can also buy someone time to try and think of the perfect thing to say. However, this often backfires, especially with the police. In defending yourself, you can inadvertently give them details pointing to motivation or put you at the location. People that know what they are doing know to let people hang themselves on their words. It does not matter if you are innocent; if they are suspicious or do not like you, they will implicate you and work backward. When dealing with people in power, it's better to be quiet.

A common method is to repeat the question. Sometimes this can be used to clarify, but when the question is yes or no, or potentially very serious, it sounds odd.

- *Did you use rat poison to try and kill my dog?*

- *Did I use rat poison to try and kill your dog???*

This means of buying time sometimes comes out automatically because it is all our brains can muster, only once it has left the lips do people realize what an obvious tell it can be.

Lying Is Actually Uncomfortable

For your average person, the lessons and scoldings we took as children for testing out the ability to lie stuck. We hate lying, especially to people in authority, because we fear getting caught and feeling shame. Instead, our brains will find a way around this by peppering a bit of truth in the lie. Not only that, even the most narcissistic people do not think of themselves as mustache-twirling villains. Everything they do can be rationalized in their own reality. When someone confronts them about it, they are smacked with the fact that they have harmed another person.

People all want to be heroes in their stories and the idea that we might actually be the villain puts us on defense. People will twist the facts and their wording to their absolute limits to avoid being confronted by guilt.

Look at the above example, all those things could be true, the only thing that wasn't was the fact they cheated. Whether they love their partner or have a hectic schedule has no bearing on the yes or no question of "did you cheat." It is all superfluous information to try and get the liar to taint the facts with emotions. This is called a *convincing statement*. This is actually normally pretty effective in getting people off your back provided you include an answer to the yes or no question.

By including elements of truth, your body language will not betray the words coming out of your mouth. If you keep it brief then your average person will be inclined to believe you. Do with that information what you will.

Look for the Unnecessary Modifiers

Thanks to the discomfort most people have with telling an outright lie they may subconsciously add a modifier to clear their conscience. It might sound obvious, but a lot of guilty people fall into this trap. Listen to the first words they say that indirectly say that they aren't telling you everything.

- *Honestly-*

- *Well, the thing is-*

- *What I CAN tell you-*

- *You see-*

- *Technically speaking-*

- *Welllllll-*

People will also twist the facts to their absolute limits to technically remain truthful.

- *Did you steal my lunch out of the work fridge?*

A truthful answer would sound more like:

- *No, I didn't!*

Even a simple "no" will suffice. However, a potentially dishonest answer would look like:

- *I would never try to steal!*

- *Technically I found it, but his name wasn't on it!*

- *I don't even like chicken salad!*

- *Did anyone see me steal it?*

All of these answers tweak the meaning to try and get around the truth without outright lying. Also there was no mention of the lunch in question. People are conscious of their discomfort and feel that if they add a modifier, that will clear them (technically, really, I don't think). In reality, this should send an alarm bell ringing to start focusing on this person.

Look for the Leaks

It's not just the words people say when they try to lie. Even if they have those mastered, their body language often gives away a few clues. Remember to look for the sudden signs of stress at pointed questions. The body may betray the lie because it is difficult to pick your words carefully and watch your body language simultaneously.

One phenomenon is called *duper's delight*. It is the appearance of a smirk when a person tells a lie they think they are nailing. If someone is lying with purpose, the thrill of getting one over on someone is profoundly satisfying, and they may smile a bit as a result. Some people smile in discomfort, so this might be something to look for at a baseline.

Another desynchronization is when a person says yes or no, but their head shake is the opposite of that answer. The person deals with three channels, the truth in their head, the lie coming out of their mouth, and how the body is engaged.

When people lie, they might try and put on a show with their body language to show that they are engaged and taking the questions seriously. Plus, a person remaining stiff as a board will definitely arouse suspicion. Trying to match the yes or no gesture and the mouth when keeping track of a lie is like rubbing your stomach and patting your head simultaneously.

The Ethical Guide to Gaslighting

Gaslighting is a word that has lost all meaning today. It is not just lying; it is fooling a person into questioning their own reality. Memories are fickle things. They are notoriously unreliable in court and can be called into doubt very easily. A very common deflection tactic that is difficult to dispute can sound like this:

- *I never said that*
- *I don't remember it that way*

- *You imagined that*
- *You heard wrong*

Unless you have evidence or another witness to the contrary this can kill a weak argument. Gaslighting is a pretty extreme measure and there is risk involved in using it. It is something that must be used sparingly, if you are caught trying to lie, it will destroy a person's trust in you. People obviously hate being lied to and if the wrong person becomes privy to that information, you will have a reputation you will never be able to escape.

- The fewer people there are that can possibly dispute you the better. Unless you are Jim Jones there is strength in numbers and a witness can cast doubt on your story and break the spell easily.

- The thing you are trying to hide has to be out of character for you. If there is a rumor that you stole money from a coworker's purse and you already have a reputation for stealing everyone's lunches out of the work fridge, gaslighting is way less effective. If you are a bit awkward, maybe not the best dressed and you moonlight as a male stripper, that is a lot easier to talk your way out of.

- If there is an overwhelming amount of evidence like a video of you with your very recognizable tattoo present or if you have an easily identifiable speech pattern trying to gaslight may result in you looking petulant.

- Some people are very confident in their opinions. We live in a post-truth world and they might not be susceptible to having their reality questioned no matter how credible your story sounds. Gaslighting them might not be effective, you will have to change tact and discredit them.

In Case of Emergency, Turn on Your Gaslight

Madeline reaps the benefits of her professionalism. She is respected at her white-collar job, doesn't rock the boat with her coworkers, and is known for being competent but a little mousy. Little do her coworkers know, Madeline has a bit of a scandalous side. She earns extra money as a model, and we are not talking about classy runways. Her private Instagram is filled with pictures of her in various stages of undress.

While she gravitates towards shoots that are more artistic than sexual, her coworkers would never know the difference; after all, she is naked in most of the pictures. She is proud of her work, but she knows that the general public would mark her with a scarlet letter if they found out. Not to mention her parents would be mortified.

She takes every precaution under the sun to keep her alter-ego a secret. Her modeling profile is wholly separate and locked down. She only accepts followers that are in the industry. She goes by a pseudonym even after correspondence with the artists and has completely segregated all forms of communication to book work. After all this, she was horrified when a male coworker named Brad showed up at her desk with a smirk on his face.

"So what do you like to do after work?" He inquired.

"I go home, feed the cat, and crochet," countered Madeline.

"Really? Well I stumbled across a very interesting picture and the girl in it looks a lot like you."

"There are a lot of pictures on the internet, you will have to be way more specific than that."

"Well, it was of you, looking very sexy in that lacy black lingerie looking back at me with beautiful bedroom eyes, gotta say I didn't think you had it in you! If I didn't have a girlfriend I might take you up on that look you were giving me."

Madeline immediately knew what he was talking about; pictures of her recent boudoir shoot had just dropped on the photographer's page, gaining a lot of traction. Still, she knew she had plausible deniability. Her pseudonym was the only identifier. Editing, glamorous makeup, and lighting can serve as a bit of a disguise. Also, her biggest ally is her appearance at work. She dressed like a librarian, her hair was always in a messy bun, and she was soft-spoken. She knew she had to stay calm despite Brad's smarmy grin getting on her nerves.

While the impulse to outright deny and try and overwhelm him with contradictions was there, she did not want to look defensive. Not only would it serve to confirm his suspicion, but that sort of reaction is what people like Brad thrive on. She did not know what he had planned with that information, and she was not keen to find out.

She knew she had to accomplish a few things:

- Make sure she did not slip up and try to deny specific details of the photos unless he was stupid enough to show them to her. She has to act as if she has never seen the photo even though she was in it.

- Make Brad question if it was truly her in the photo. Once again she had plausible deniability on her side but a photo he can refer to might be a bit tricky.

- Do her best to shorten the conversation. The more she has to talk the more defensive she will look plus any slip-up will be fuel on her professional funeral pyre.

- If all fails, discredit Brad to ensure no one believes him. She has a small window of opportunity. If Brad starts circulating the pictures and other people agree with him, she is finished in the company and she likes having a salary and health insurance. She had to nip this in the bud.

"You walked across the building to tell me you look at lingerie photos on the internet," Madeline inquired. She knew she had to be calm, and most of all — boring.

"C'mon you don't have to hide your little side hustle from me!" Brad doubled down.

"Do I look like a model to you?"

"Now you do."

"That's hard to believe since I have never modeled for anything before." Madeline said flatly. Her blasé reaction to a coworker seeing her in a compromising photo confused Brad. Madeline could see his cage was rattled by not letting him see her squirm. But his frown revealed something else, frustration and he pulled out his phone in defiance.

"Don't tell me that's not you!" He said defiantly.

"That doesn't even look like me," Madeline said putting on a confused face, she knew she could not recoil from the picture instead she confidently brought it closer to her face.

"Just admit it or I'm going to start showing this little number off to everyone," Brad said looking more and more frustrated. Perfect.

"Have fun with that." She avoided defensive cliches like:

- *No one will believe you!*

- *It's your word against mine!*

- *You can't do that!*

She had to sound completely unbothered because that is how a person who was falsely accused of something so absurd would behave up until a point. She could tell it was working since his smug smile was replaced with a frown and red cheeks. He was embarrassed now but people like Brad are very hesitant to admit they are wrong.

"Maybe we can ask someone else if they agree with me." Brad stated, it's now or never.

"You're creeping me out Brad, I don't know what to tell you, that's not me. If you want to take the photo over to Patricia in HR you can do that. Maybe she can tell you if this woman looks like me. Also, I don't think your girlfriend would appreciate you seeking out women in scandalous pictures."

Madeline had to call his bluff right then and there before more people got involved. Patricia was the logical choice, not only is she a person that has power over Brad, but she and Patricia exchanged crocheting patterns and cat videos. She would never believe Brad and would not take kindly to him bullying her work buddy and showing her scantily clad pictures.

"Whatever, I know your secret." Brad walked away.

Madeline had won this battle but she had to win the war. She realized that Brad showed her the photo on the photographer's social media account, not a screenshot. She saw Brad had liked the picture so she took a screenshot of that to use against Brad in case he tried anything like this again. His girl would likely get a kick out of it. For good measure, she texted the photographer and asked her to take down the photo and replace it with someone that looked similar. Since odds are he did not keep a copy, if he tried to hunt down the picture he would be confronted with someone who was definitely different. The photographer gladly obliged and they had a good laugh about the situation. Madeline also blocked Brad and texted all her photographer friends to do the same and paused her profile so he could not search for it. She can start it up again after a week or two once things cooled down and a social media break was warranted anyway.

Madeline decided to keep her head down at work but continued to watch Brad. She noticed him looking at her with a very annoyed expression. It was safe to assume that he could not access the photo again. With all her bases covered, he was successfully gaslit but she needed to make him pay for trying to blackmail her. With her secret safe she joked about the exchange with anyone that asked why Brad got so heated with her. She searched her own name in front of them only to find a profile filled with innocuous photos of her family and memes. Everyone side-eyed Brad for the stunt and he got a visit from Patricia for harassing a female employee with inappropriate photos.

To protect yourself, you may have to lie and get really good at it. If the wrong person catches you leaving a strip club or a Furry convention, they are likely to try and use that potentially compromising information to discredit or blackmail you. Things that should have no bearing on your professional life can be weaponized against you. If they have proof they are likely to flaunt it at the first sign of resistance if they don't do so right away. When a person says "I saw you there" a simple "No you didn't" will suffice. As we learned, word vomit can look overcompensating and you don't want to introduce unnecessary details that can be contradicted. Acting unaffected by an accusation and limited evidence takes away the person's power over you.

I'll Do What I Want, Not What You Tell Me!

Reverse psychology is a beautiful tool for demanding people. From children to childish adults, it works by tapping into our defiance. This is due to the psychological phenomenon called *reactance*. We resent others telling us we can't do something or have something. Certain people will actively defy expectations to feel like they have control. People can be blinded into thinking they have control over an outcome when in reality, that outcome is predetermined or entirely out of their control. This quirk of human psychology can make a person surprisingly malleable as long as you don't mind them thinking they are seizing control.

As we discussed in the gaslighting section, people take glee in discovering a secret and love to hear a person beg for discretion. Thanks to the *Streisand Effect,* this can end in disaster. This is when desperately trying to bury a truth or dispute something ends with you bringing more attention to the subject. A famous example of this would be when the Church of Scientology attempted to censor a particularly unhinged video of Tom Cruise getting interviewed by Oprah. Their attempt to conceal the video only made people want to see it more. It eventually became a meme with late-night talk shows mocking it and all manner of edits circling around the internet. If you're going to hide something, shut up about it; don't tell people not to look.

An excellent way to influence kids with a bit of reverse psychology is by giving them an illusion of choice. Let's say you need the kid to stop playing and clean up. Something that can lead to a tantrum would be:

- *Time for bed, put the toys away!*

Since the kid feels like they have no choice they have a breakdown. Instead try something like:

- *Do you want to help mommy by putting the teddy bear away or picking up the blocks?*

There is no sudden shift in tone and it opens the door to proceed with the routine. Adults don't give children enough credit. They have agency, freewill and stubbornness they probably picked up from their parents. They also like to feel important by being asked to help. Think about how you would like to be spoken to, if someone was always giving you commands you would get pretty cranky too!

A technique used by therapists is called *Motivational Interviewing*. This is asking a series of leading questions to get an otherwise resistant person to see the benefits of something difficult. Let's say a person is really addicted to alcohol but they insist they have it under control. They might be asked about their recent problems (suspended license, unemployment, kids won't speak to them), how they feel about them, and their fears. Therapists are great at getting to the root of issues because they can take these complex thoughts and label them with emotions despite the interviewee never acknowledging their feelings.

- *That sounds extremely frustrating.*

- *You sound very saddened by what happened.*

- *It is understandable that you are angry with this person.*

- *You sound very guilty about that.*

Then they pick at the cause of all these problems, at this point all signs point to the alcohol or a direct consequence of the alcohol. That's when they are hit with the stinger, what can the person do to change the current track of their life. The therapist made it so the person had agency in improving their life when originally they could not see reason.

What Have We Learned?

- Your average person is a terrible liar. Use that to your advantage by looking for signs of stress timed with specific questions. Remembering should lead to further investigation, not direct accusation.

- People will talk and talk to try and get out of trouble, never interrupt your enemy when he is making a mistake.

- When you need to gaslight, less is more, never look defensive or angry.

- Getting difficult people to do things with minimal drama is a wonderful thing. Reverse psychology gives people a sense of agency while still doing what you want.

IS IT MORALLY RIGHT TO USE DARK PSYCHOLOGY?

"Well, my family can't live in good intentions Marge!"

- NED FLANDERS

We have learned a lot and even had a lot of fun on this journey but there is one thing we have been kind of avoiding when it comes to using dark psychology; is any of this actually okay?

It's a tough reflection to look at; you might see a lot of the behaviors of people that have harmed you in this advice. You may be realizing that someone you care about has manipulated you in the past. It can be hurtful, but this advice can be helpful and you have probably engaged in dark psychology in the past, even if you did not know the words for it.

Relax, You Have Probably Done All This Before

If you look at yourself, you know you have lied in the past. Since we all think we have impeachable character, we rationalize those lies. We all lie about Santa because it is a rite of passage for children who celebrate Christmas. Schools participate and even the government participates in it because it's fun. However, if a parent told you that he tells his children that a coyote in a pink collar left sandwiches under their child's pillow for their birthday, you might think it's bonkers. There is no difference except that one lie has been reinforced by society.

We lie to people all the time to protect ourselves. We tell people "I'm fine" when we aren't because we don't want our reality to bleed into theirs. We think of it as being kind but we are still lying. We tell our friends that we love them, that they are trustworthy, and that we would come to them with anything, meaningless words that only serve to reinforce the relationship without anyone having to do any work.

We lie to protect other people's feelings as well. Whether it's because of insecurity in the relationship or not wanting to deal with any emotional labor we will say a lot of things to keep the peace. You may not like a friend's new significant other; you may see behavior that bothers them, but you rationalize in your head that it is not your place. You keep up a facade that you accept this new person when it's not the truth. You tell a person you are not angry or saddened by a choice they made, not only robbing them of any opportunity to re-examine the choice but enabling them to do it again.

Now you might be telling yourself, fine I have done those things but those things only hurt me or they were innocent, I've never actually hurt anyone. You might be wrong about that one too.

The World Is Not Fair

Most things in this world are finite, and for you to gain, inevitably, someone is bound to lose out. Let's say you used the advice in this book to land a great job. Well, in the decision to hire you, there was also a pool of people who were discarded. Odds are, they had similar qualifications; the law of averages states some of them might have had a more challenging life or might have needed the job more. What sets you apart? Maybe you were the best and most qualified, but another factor was that you just knew how to package yourself better.

Remember, the interview stage is just a giant social exercise to ensure you fit in. You knew to laugh at the interviewer's jokes, sell your strengths without appearing smug, reframe your weaknesses, and mirror the interviewer. Turning up the charm above baseline is dishonest when you think about it. Whether interviewing for sales, janitorial duties, back-of-house development, creative, or management, these skills are only beneficial in an interview, even if they have no bearing on the job. If you had not employed any of this advice, someone else might have gotten the job; would that have been fairer?

Before you resolve to be the nicest, most open, generous person to walk the earth since Christ himself, slow down. Remember, the world is not fair, and this would be the equivalent of bringing a pool noodle to a gunfight. Agreeable people make less money than non-agreeable people. Why? Because in trying to get ahead in the world, you have to ask tough questions, sell yourself and trust everyone at their word. If you don't question management's judgment and ask for that raise, you will never get it. If you don't prop yourself over another person, that person will walk all over you. Making your life an open book to always remain honest opens you to getting exploited.

You might feel guilty at the moment but remember this; most people would do the same thing. There are entire books and seminar series based around navigating job interviews or sales, predicated on exploiting human psychology. At the very least, being aware of these skills can keep you safe from all the narcissistic abusers in this world, sleazy salespeople, and those who would try and take advantage of kindness. Unless it involves details of the date of your conception, there is no such thing as too much information. Having this and knowing when to use it discreetly can only help you. People with black-and-white thinking will never be able to use this information properly. It takes empathy and even kindness to make this work to make you into a happier and better person.

Using Dark Psychology for Good

Think about all the times your life has improved because you used dark psychology. Your new job increased the quality of life for you and your family. Maybe you are a more confident version of yourself, taking more risks and reaping more rewards. Did you help a friend by reframing an issue they were having? Or maybe the personal training services you sold by pulling every sales trick in the book have had impressive results. Hell, maybe you just had a more relaxing night by using reverse psychology on a child who didn't want to go to bed. Dark psychology may be keeping you safe by being aware of all the tricks people use to weasel their way into you or a friend's life.

You might be starting to see the world a bit differently now. You are revisiting old gossip videos and are able to pick up on classic stress indicators and lies. You might see right through a sales pitch or know to recognize how you might get sucked into group think and catch yourself.

Just because you have this knowledge doesn't mean you will turn into Jim Jones or Elizabeth Holmes. You are just now a savvier version of yourself. If you go on to use this information to exploit those with self-esteem then that is not a reflection of the knowledge, that is a reflection of you. But, if you make a name for yourself, build influence and then use that influence for good, then you are just using the tools provided to you.

CONCLUSION

Dark psychology can be a scary, yet wonderful thing. The ability to read people on the fly, spot scams, sell anything, get ahead at work, and smooth out disagreements will take you far in life.

Some people could only dream of having the awareness to have these skills. While just reading about what makes humans tick will not make you a master, knowing what to look for and what to practice will develop your skills.

Most of these skills boil down to being a nice person with a backbone. You don't have to stoop down at the level of those who may have harmed you before. You can still go on to be a great, successful person by bringing dark psychology into the light.

Effective communication, putting people at ease with confidence and sensing friction with a glance will just make you a great person to be around. You might even become a positive influence in other people's lives.

Will you have to lie sometimes, or hide certain things to protect yourself? Yes. While it sounds cynical, if you picked up this book you might already have had an experience where you have been manipulated in the past.

You may have been lied to, taken advantage of, robbed, or traumatized. Odds are, this might happen again. If it does, give yourself grace for finding yourself in a similar situation and get ready. Be quiet and observe.

Hopefully, you will never have to dance in the palm of someone's hand again. You will not only see it coming, but you might even be able to turn the tables. Stand up straight, open your eyes and listen.

I CAN SEE YOU'RE THE KIND
OF PERSON WHO GETS THINGS DONE

Did you know that you are in the top percent of readers in the world? You committed to reading a book and made it through to the end. Congratulations for having and exercising your *get things done mindset*!

Seeing as you're a person who gets things done, could you do me a small favor and leave a short book review?

Scan the applicable QR Code below with your phone *(on camera mode)*, to take you directly to your Amazon review page. Log into your account *(if you haven't already that is)* and in less than a minute from now, it'll be done.

Amazon US Review

Amazon UK Review

If you don't have the time now, then that's no problem at all. Remember to download your 2 free bonus eBooks before you leave.

REFERENCES

American Murder: The Family Next Door | Netflix Official Site. (2020). Www.netflix.com. https://www.netflix.com/title/81130130

Arkowitz, H., Miller, W. R., & Rollnick, S. (2017). *Motivational interviewing in the treatment of psychological problems.* The Guilford Press.

Aviezer, H., Trope, Y., & Todorov, A. (2012). Body Cues, Not Facial Expressions, Discriminate Between Intense Positive and Negative Emotions. *Science, 338*(6111), 1225–1229. https://doi.org/10.1126/science.1224313

REFERENCES

Bailey, L. (2022, July 25). *Interview with an Editor in Advertising* [Letter to J A].

Bavelas, J., Kenwood, C., Johnson, T., & Phillips, B. (2002). An experimental study of when and how speakers use gestures to communicate. *Gesture*, *2*(1), 1–17. https://doi.org/10.1075/gest.2.1.02bav

Borau, S. (2016, January). *The advertising performance of non-ideal female models as a function of viewers' body mass index: A moderated mediation analysis of two competing affective pathways*. International Journal of Advertising.

Burgo, J. (2016). *The narcissist you know*. Touchstone, An Imprint Of Simon & Schuster, Inc.

Byrne, D., & Nelson, D. (1965). Attraction as a linear function of proportion of positive reinforcements. *Journal of Personality and Social Psychology*, *1*(6), 659–663. https://doi.org/10.1037/h0022073

REFERENCES

Camu, J. N. (2013, January 30). *Mirroring: A calculated therapeutic technique or just conversation?* Dr. Camu. http://www.fuelforemotionalhealth.com/2013/01/mirroring-a-calculated-therapeutic-technique-or-just-conversation/

Carreyrou, J. (2019). *BAD BLOOD : secrets and lies in a silicon valley startup.* Vintage.

Chan, D., Fitzsimmons, C. M., Mandler, M. D., & Batista, P. J. (2021). Ten simple rules for acing virtual interviews. *PLOS Computational Biology*, *17*(6), e1009057. https://doi.org/10.1371/journal.pcbi.1009057

Chartrand, T. L., & Bargh, J. A. (1999). The chameleon effect: The perception-behavior link and social interaction. *Journal of Personality and Social*

Psychology, *76*(6), 893–910. https://doi.org/10.1037//0022-3514.76.6.893

Dreeke, R., & Stauth, C. (2022). *Sizing people up : a veteran FBI agent's user manual for behavior prediction*. John Murray Learning.

Edwards, J., & Brunson, R. (2018). *Copywriting secrets : how everyone can use the power of words to get more clicks, sales, and profits-- no matter what you sell or who you sell it to!* Author Academy Elite.

Fisher, R., & Ury, W. (2012). *Getting To Yes: Negotiating An Agreement Without Giving In*. Random House Business Books.

Fredrickson, B. L. (2001). The role of positive emotions in positive psychology: The broaden-and-build theory of positive emotions. *American Psychologist*, *56*(3), 218–226. https://doi.org/10.1037//0003-066x.56.3.218

Fuselier, W., & Lf. (1981). *A Practical Guide for Hostage Negotiation*. National Criminal Justice Reference Service. https://www.ojp.gov/pdffiles1/Digitization/78332 NCJRS.pdf

Gj Thompson, & Jb Jenkins. (2004). *Verbal judo : the gentle art of persuasion, rev. ed.* Quill.

Guinn, J. (2018). *The road to Jonestown : Jim Jones and Peoples Temple*. Simon & Schuster Paperbacks, An Imprint Of Simon & Schuster, Inc.

Heck, P. R., & Krueger, J. I. (2016). Social Perception of Self-Enhancement Bias and Error. *Social Psychology*, *47*(6), 327–339. https://doi.org/10.1027/1864-9335/a000287

Higgins, C. A., & Judge, T. A. (2004). The Effect of Applicant Influence Tactics on Recruiter Perceptions of Fit and Hiring Recommendations: A

Field Study. *Journal of Applied Psychology, 89*(4), 622–632. https://doi.org/10.1037/0021-9010.89.4.622

Hughes, J. (2009). A PILOT STUDY OF NATURALLY OCCURRING HIGH-PROBABILITY REQUEST SEQUENCES IN HOSTAGE NEGOTIATIONS. *Journal of Applied Behavior Analysis, 42*(2), 491–496. https://doi.org/10.1901/jaba.2009.42-491

Jacob, C. (2011). Retail salespeople's mimicry of customers: Effects on consumer behavior. *Journal of Retailing and Consumer Services.*

JCS - Criminal Psychology. (n.d.-a). *Jennifer's Solution.* Www.youtube.com. Retrieved August 7, 2022, from https://www.youtube.com/watch?v=UQt46gvYO40&t=1106s

REFERENCES

JCS - Criminal Psychology. (n.d.-b). *The Curious Case of Dalia Dippolito*. Www.youtube.com. Retrieved August 7, 2022, from https://www.youtube.com/watch?v=7JttwV6XZ_I &t=9s

JCS - Criminal Psychology. (2019, January 17). *The Case of Chris Watts*. YouTube. https://www.youtube.com/watch?v=Xfg861hO-Ag

JCS - Criminal Psychology. (2020, December). *Wrath of Jodi*. Www.youtube.com. https://www.youtube.com/watch?v=N274EurzpA A&t=1480s

Joss Fong. (2012, December 7). *Eye-Opener: Why Do Pupils Dilate in Response to Emotional States?* Scientific American. https://www.scientificamerican.com/article/eye-opener-why-do-pupils-dialate/

REFERENCES

Judge, T. A., Livingston, B. A., & Hurst, C. (2012). Do nice guys—and gals—really finish last? The joint effects of sex and agreeableness on income. *Journal of Personality and Social Psychology*, *102*(2), 390–407. https://doi.org/10.1037/a0026021

MacDonald, G., Nail, P. R., & Harper, J. R. (2011). Do people use reverse psychology? An exploration of strategic self-anticonformity. *Social Influence*, *6*(1), 1–14. https://doi.org/10.1080/15534510.2010.517282

Marcotte, B. (2018). *Using data science to tell which of these people is lying*.

Murphy, N. A. (2007). Appearing Smart: The Impression Management of Intelligence, Person Perception Accuracy, and Behavior in Social Interaction. *Personality and Social Psychology Bulletin*, *33*(3),

325–339.

https://doi.org/10.1177/0146167206294871

Murphy, N. A., Hall, J. A., & Colvin, C. R. (2003). Accurate Intelligence Assessments in Social Interactions: Mediators and Gender Effects. *Journal of Personality*, *71*(3), 465–493. https://doi.org/10.1111/1467-6494.7103008

NLP Modeling, finding the structure of excellence. (2011, May 8). NLP Mentor. https://nlp-mentor.com/nlp-modeling/

Rand, R. (2018). *The Menendez murders : the shocking untold story of the Menendez family and the killings that stunned the nation.* Benbella Books, Inc.

Robbins, T. (2021, February 12). *5 most effective neuro linguistic programming techniques.* Tonyrobbins.com.

REFERENCES

https://www.tonyrobbins.com/leadership-impact/nlp-techniques/

Ronningstam, E. (n.d.). *Narcissistic Personality Disorder: Guide for Providers at McLean Hospital.* Www.mcleanhospital.org. https://www.mcleanhospital.org/npd-provider-guide

Sanders, T. (2006). *The likeability factor : how to boost your L-factor & achieve your life's dreams.* Three Rivers Press, C.

Sezer, O., Gino, F., & Norton, M. I. (2018). Humblebragging: A distinct—and ineffective—self-presentation strategy. *Journal of Personality and Social Psychology, 114*(1), 52–74. https://doi.org/10.1037/pspi0000108

REFERENCES

Solanto, M. V. (2011). *Cognitive-behavioral therapy for adult ADHD : targeting executive dysfunction.* Guilford Press.

Stout, M. (2022). *OUTSMARTING THE SOCIOPATH NEXT DOOR : how to protect yourself against a ruthless manipulator.* Harmony Crown.

Twenge, J. M., & W Keith Campbell. (2013). *The narcissism epidemic : living in the age of entitlement.* Atria Paperback.

van Baaren, R. B., Holland, R. W., Steenaert, B., & van Knippenberg, A. (2003). Mimicry for money: Behavioral consequences of imitation. *Journal of Experimental Social Psychology, 39*(4), 393–398. https://doi.org/10.1016/s0022-1031(03)00014-3

Word, C. O., Zanna, M. P., & Cooper, J. (1974). The nonverbal mediation of self-fulfilling prophecies in interracial interaction. *Journal of Experimental*

REFERENCES

Social Psychology, *10*(2), 109–120. https://doi.org/10.1016/0022-1031(74)90059-6

Zhu, R., & Argo, J. J. (2013). Exploring the Impact of Various Shaped Seating Arrangements on Persuasion. *Journal of Consumer Research*, *40*(2), 336–349. https://doi.org/10.1086/670392

Made in United States
Orlando, FL
17 January 2023

28757702R00125